For This

Cause

I Bow

My

Knees

For This Cause I Bow My Knees

A Moving Testament

REKESHA PITTMAN

REIGNAISSANCE PUBLICATIONS

ISBN 978-0-9820158-5-8

Printed in the United States of America by Reignaissance™ Publications.

Cover Design: Robert J. Connor

Assistant Editor: Crystal Daniels

Book Formatting: Tabitha D. Spencer-Asare

CAUSES

*Thank You LORD
for allowing me to be a vessel.*

*To my husband,
Matthew A. Pittman,
for supporting my dreams,
embracing the vision,
and praying me through.*

INTRODUCTION

My Soul is a Witness

I have witnessed the transforming power of God. He has allowed me to minister the Word through movement and see captives set free, souls delivered, and healing manifested. The Lord has gifted me with the ability to teach and to see lives cleansed by the washing of the Word.

The following pages are but a small reflection of the passion that I have to deliver the Word of God effectively and inspirationally. My journey in the dance and movement ministries has been filled with awe, wonder, and rejoicing evermore as He continues to order my every step.

When we live, move, and have our being in Him, He will give us the hunger we need to seek to have an understanding of His Word. The ability to properly convey His Living Word through movement is not solely for our benefit, but also to impact the lives of others forever.

The Bible instructs us in Proverbs 4:7 *"Wisdom is the principal thing; Therefore get wisdom. And in all your getting, get understanding."*

There is a surplus of information available to us now concerning the dance ministry. With the availability of many books, newsletters, DVDs, audio teachings, and the internet, we are without excuse. We must seize the opportunity to grow in our ministries so that we can continue to go into all the world and preach the Gospel.

Edification, wisdom, and even correction is the order of the day for all of us. The small slice of revelation He has given me is activated by what He has placed inside of you. It is my prayer that the Lord opens the eyes of our understanding, so that we may comprehend the magnitude of His love for us.

Whatever your area of assignment is in the ministry of movement, do it all to the glory of God. Lack of knowledge will cause us to perish if we are not showing ourselves approved by devoted study. This is the time when all worship artists must know the Lord personally.

Step inside these pages and allow the Lord to transition you from the natural to the supernatural. It is my prayer that you are not inspired to teach like I do, but to obtain your very own unique revelation of truth that He has reserved just for you. Be inspired to move afresh, full of life and creativity!

Forever His Servant,

Rekesha Pittman

CAUSE 1

SHALL WE DANCE?
An Old Testament Investigation

Dance is present throughout the Old Testament Scriptures. Dance was used in many ways and for various reasons, but it cannot be argued that dance does not have a place in the Bible. Dance was often a means of response, often accompanied by musical instruments and lyrical songs. The Word shows dance being done by men, women and children. It was embraced and utilized by a king and a prophetess. Dance was an individual as well as a corporate experience.

We find the first representation of dance in the Bible through Miriam in Exodus 15:20, *"Then Miriam the prophetess, the sister of Aaron, took the timbrel in her hand; and all the women went out after her with timbrels and <u>with dances</u>."* This is the first of several Scriptures that mention dance specifically by name. There are several Old Testament Scriptures that also refer to dance specifically: Exodus 32:19, Judges 11:34, Judges 21:21-23, 1 Samuel 18:6-7, 1 Samuel 21:11, 1 Samuel 29:5, 1 Samuel 30:16, 2 Samuel 6:14-16, Job 21:11, Psalm 30:11, Psalm 149:3, Psalm 150:4, Ecclesiastes 3:4, Jeremiah 31:4, Jeremiah 31:13, and Lamentations 5:15.

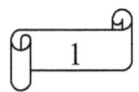

SHALL WE DANCE?

In the Hebrew, there are many words that may be able to give us a deeper understanding of the original meaning of the authors. In The New Strong's® Exhaustive Concordance of the Bible, we find a few words that expressly mention dance:

Karar (3769) to dance (whirl about)

Machowl (4234) a round dance

Mechowlah (4245) a dance

There are also Scriptures that do not specifically include the word "dance" but their meaning implies its use. Often, the word "rejoice" is indicative of the dance. Anne Stevenson, author of **Restoring the Dance** states, "The single best overall definition I have found for the word rejoice is 'the act of expressing joy.' It seems it would be impossible to rejoice without any type of action or expression." (Stevenson 55) Some Hebrew words associated with dance that include rejoice are:

Giyl or **Guwl** (1523) to spin round (under the influence of any violent emotion), i.e. usually rejoice, or (as cringing) fear: be glad, joy, be joyful, rejoice

Alaz (5937) to jump for joy, i.e. exult- be joyful, rejoice, triumph

Alats (5970) to jump for joy, exult- be joyful, rejoice, triumph

There are other expressions of movement that are linked with dance in the Old Testament Scriptures. Upon further study in the Hebrew, we also find the following words related to movement:

Barak (1288) to kneel, to bless God (as an act of adoration)

Dalag (1801) to spring: leap

Chagag (2287) to move in a circle, to march in a sacred procession, to observe a festival, to be giddy: celebrate, dance, reel to and fro

Yadah (3034) to use (hold out) the hand, to revere or worship (with extended hands)

Nathar (5425) to jump, i.e. be violently agitated, to terrify, shake off, untie- drive asunder, leap, (let) loose: make, move, undo

Pazaz (6339) solidify (as if by refining); also to spring (as if separating the limbs): leap, be made strong

Raqad (7540) to stamp, i.e. to spring about (wildly or for joy): dance, jump, leap, skip.

Shachah (7812) to depress, prostrate (in homage to royalty or God): bow (self) down, crouch, fall down (flat), make to stoop, worship

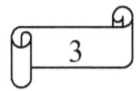

SHALL WE DANCE?

Towdah (8426) an extension of the hand, (usually) adoration; a choir of Worshippers

From the aforementioned studies, we are able to get a foundation for the understanding of dance as it was used in the Old Testament. Through a study of the Scriptures we find that dance was not just done for the sake of dancing. Dance was symbolic and purposeful. There are several themes that are present with the demonstration of dance in the Old Testament.

Celebration

"Now it had happened as they were coming home, when David was returning from the slaughter of the Philistine, that the women had come out of all the cities of Israel, singing and dancing, to meet King Saul, with tambourines, with joy, and with musical instruments." (1 Samuel 18:6) Here we see dance as a response to the defeat of one and the victory of another. We know that God has already won the victory, so celebration is very much an appropriate demonstration of dance in the church today.

Greeting

When Jephthah came to his house at Mizpah, there was his daughter, coming out to meet him with timbrels and dancing; and she was his only child... (Judges 11:34a) We can greet our heavenly Father in His house (or sanctuary)

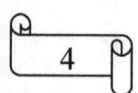
4

FOR THIS CAUSE I BOW MY KNEES

with instruments of praise to welcome Him in. This can be exercised today by dancers who minister during times of praise and worship in the church setting.

Prophecy

So the women sang as they danced, and said: "Saul has slain his thousands, And David his ten thousands. (1 Samuel 18:7) As described by Dr. Aimee Kovacs in *Dancing Into the Anointing*, "This was a prophetic dance. David had not yet slain his ten thousands. This prophetic dance was one of the reasons Saul persecuted David." (Kovacs 11) We can use dance prophetically today as well. It is important that we seek the Lord's will in this area so that we are not demonstrating our own desires, but the proceeding Word of God.

Joy and Restoration

"Again I will build you, and you shall be rebuilt, O virgin of Israel! You shall again be adorned with your tambourines, and shall go forth in the dances of those who rejoice." (Jeremiah 31:4) We can dance to celebrate the dedication of life to Christ, or the restoration of a fallen brother or sister in the Lord. We can use dance after an altar call or other appropriate time in the worship service as directed.

Praise and Worship

We still face some opposition in the church setting today in regards to dance. I am glad that the Lord reminds us to *"Let them praise His name with the dance."* (Psalm 149:3a) He then tells us to *"Praise Him with the timbrel and dance."* (Psalm 150:4a) King David demonstrated praise and worship in dance with abandon in 2 Samuel 6:14a which reads, *"Then David danced before the Lord with all his might..."* as David and the people were bringing up the Ark of the Covenant. This is a wonderful example for the people of God, as it encourages public demonstration of the dance.

2 Samuel also instructs us that our dances are to be offered as praise to the Lord, and not for the approval of the observers. We see in the Scriptures that dance is also a congregational opportunity according to Jeremiah 31:13: *"Then shall the virgin rejoice in the dance, and the young men and the old, together; for I will turn their mourning to joy, will comfort them, and make them rejoice rather than sorrow."* We know that dance is not limited by gender, age, or title. We are seeing more men stepping forward in the church today in both combined gender dance ministries, as well as men's dance and movement groups.

Instrumental

There are several Scriptures that remind us that dance frequently works in conjunction with instruments and singing.

"The singers went before, the players on instruments followed after; among them were the maidens playing timbrels."
Psalm 68:25

"Is this not David, of whom they sang to one another in dances..."
1 Samuel 29:5a

"Raise a song and strike the timbrel."
Psalm 81:2a

Today we are seeing that more Worship Arts Departments in churches are beginning to include dance as a regular, ongoing part of the service. Dancers are participating during Praise Team and choir music selections, instrumental presentations in worship gatherings, concerts, and special programs. We are not limited concerning our opportunities to dance before the Lord.

Lord of the Dance

The Lord knows very well the power and effectiveness of music and movement working together. We find the Lord's use of it in the Scripture: *"And in every place where the staff of punishment passes, which the LORD lays on*

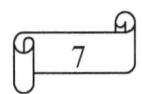

SHALL WE DANCE?

him, it will be with tambourines and harps; and in battles of brandishing He will fight with it."
-Isaiah 30:32

It is exciting to see that the Lord uses music in warfare! When we use dance as warfare today, we know according to the Word that it is the Lord Who approves it for battle.

The most important lesson that is learned from studying Old Testament examples is that dance is not a haphazard and meaningless activity. Dance is purposeful and directed. When dancers get an understanding of these factors, many arguments against dance in the church today will be refuted- not with words, but by demonstration. I know by experience from those who have walked up to me after ministry and said, "I was against dance in the church because I thought it was fleshly, but you have changed my mind today." How wonderful it is to know that the Lord is our Defender when we follow His pattern by living, moving, and having our being in Him!

SOURCES CITED

1. Anne Stevenson, **Restoring the Dance** (55)
2. Dr. Aimee Kovacs, ***Dancing Into the Anointing*** (11)

CAUSE 2

For This Cause
I Bow My Knees

A New Testament Dance Study

There are many people who argue that dance in the New Testament is relatively minimal. Many of the passages of Scripture that deal directly with dance have been used to state that dance no longer has a place in the worship setting today. It is interesting to note that the Word never commands us to stop dancing, as we are encouraged to *"Praise Him with the timbrel and dance."* (Psalm 150:4)

Dance in the New Testament is first mentioned in Matthew 11:17 which states, *"We played the flute for you, and you did not dance; We mourned to you, and you did not lament."* The Greek word used for dance here is **orcheomai**, which means *to dance (from the rank-like or regular motion).* "Rank-like" or "regular motion" could very well suggest that this type of dance described was orderly and done according to the traditional (regular) way. Many traditional dances include choreography or a series of steps that are characteristic to that certain dance type. Here Jesus is referring to "this generation" as those who hear, but do not respond to (or do) anything in accordance to

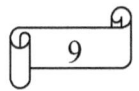

what they hear. It seems to indicate that a natural response to the playing of the flute would be to dance, but upon hearing the music this was not done. We are commanded in James 1:22 to be *"...doers of the Word, and not hearers only."* We are expected to respond according to the Word that is given.

There are other instances of dance mentioned in the New Testament as well. The most infamous mention of dance is found in both Matthew 14:6 and Mark 6:22 which describe the account of Herodias' daughter dancing before Herod. This dance took place at his birthday celebration and greatly pleased him to the point that he offered the young lady whatever she requested. The Greek word **orcheomai** is used here as well. If the dance was merely described as 'a dance,' then what makes the dance in itself the culprit?

We can infer from Scripture that dance was appropriate for times of celebration and was acceptable in the presence of the king. It also demonstrates the impact dance can make on those who witness it. It is the intention (or the heart) that makes the difference. We can conclude that this is a warning for us not to use dance (or anything else) as a means to gain special treatment from people or bring glory to ourselves. As 1 Corinthians 10:31 reminds us, *"Therefore, whether you eat or drink, or whatever you do, do all to the glory of God."*

We see dance in another place in the New Testament as well. Luke Chapter 15 illustrates the parable of the lost son who left his father's house to pursue his own desires. He realized his error, and upon returning to his father's house, a great celebration was given for the younger son to welcome his return. *"Now his older son was in the field. And as he came and drew near to the house, he heard music and dancing."* (Luke 15:25) The word for dance in the Greek here is **choros**, meaning: *a ring, round dance ("choir").* We see the correlation of music and dancing together in this scenario, and we also often rely on the use of music when we dance in the church today. We see in this account that from the original meaning of the word, this was a group of people who danced together during a time of celebration. This reminds us how much more we should celebrate with dancing when a brother or sister returns to the Father!

Expressive worship has never "gone out of style." The New Testament gives examples of physical actions coupled with worship. According to John 4:23-24, *"But the hour is coming, and now is, when the true worshipers will worship the Father in spirit and truth; for the Father is seeking such to worship Him. God is Spirit, and those who worship Him must worship in spirit and truth."* **Proskuneo** is the Greek word used here that means: *to fawn or crouch to, prostrate oneself in homage (do reverence to, adore).* Worship requires action. Satan himself even

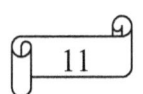

understands that worship includes a physical posture. He tried to get Jesus to worship him by bowing. We see this in Matthew 4:9-10: *"And he said to Him, 'All these things I will give You if You will fall down and worship me. Then Jesus said to him, "Away with you, Satan! For it is written, 'You shall worship the LORD your God, and Him only you shall serve.'"* By gaining an understanding of the Word, we are assured that physical worship is a New Testament activity as well.

We are to take a "leap of faith." Acts Chapters 3 and 14 share the accounts of men who had been healed from physical ailments. In Acts 3:8-9, a lame man was healed and demonstrated the results: *"So he, leaping up, stood and walked and entered the temple with them—walking, leaping, and praising God. And all the people saw him walking and praising God."* He demonstrated his healing through movement, and it was witnessed openly.

We also see leaping as an act of faith in Acts 14:8-10 which reads, *"And in Lystra a certain man without strength in his feet was sitting, a cripple from his mother's womb, who had never walked. This man heard Paul speaking. Paul, observing him intently and seeing that he had faith to be healed, said with a loud voice, "Stand up straight on your feet!" And he leaped and walked."* We can dance and leap as a sign of healing and confirmation that the Word received in faith is for us today.

It is time to get physical in our worship! The Word tells us that everyone will do so in Philippians 2:10: *"That at the name of Jesus every knee should bow, of those in heaven, and of those on earth, and of those under the earth..."* The Greek meaning for bow here is **kampto**, meaning to bend. We bend our knees and our bodies to the Lord in dance today to make the name of the Lord Jesus known in and beyond the church setting.

Though dance is often labeled as an "Old Testament" tradition, we know that the Word is true today. Physical expressions of worship are not only demonstrated in the New Testament, it is expected and understood as an outward sign of an inward belief. As a response to earthly persecutions we are instructed to *"Rejoice in that day and leap for joy! For indeed your reward is great in heaven, for in like manner their fathers did to the prophets."* (Luke 6:23)

We have been gifted with the ability to dance. When ministering gifts to one another, 1 Peter 4:10-11 gives us these guidelines: *"As each one has received a gift, minister it to one another, as good stewards of the manifold grace of God. If anyone speaks, let him speak as the oracles of God. If anyone ministers, let him do it as with the ability which God supplies, that in all things God may be glorified through Jesus Christ, to whom belong the glory and the dominion forever and ever. Amen."* The Greek word for 'minister' used here is **choregeo** (Strong's #5524) a compound word derived from the Greek words **choros** (#5525- a round dance) and **ago** (#71- to bring forth) meaning *to be a dance-leader, to furnish.* I think it not a coincidence that ministry and dance are linked in this manner. Our gifts are God-given, and belong to Him for His glory. Whether dance is considered "old" or "new," let us praise His name in it!

Source: The New Strong's Exhaustive Concordance of the Bible (1990)

CAUSE 3

$PEND AND $AVE: INVEST IN YOUR MINISTRY

We must be realistic when it comes to the politics of ministry. Though not as common as desired, there are a growing number of dance ministries being assisted by the local church with purchasing ministry garments, worship instruments, flags, banners, group travel expenses, conference registrations, educational materials, and other ministry needs. This is an ideal situation in which the church realizes the value of the movement ministry as a partner in spreading the Gospel.

The reality for many ministries is that they are responsible for paying the full cost of ministry participation. Often, this results in debates about the cost of garments, ownership questions, outside ministry participation, and rights and responsibilities. We will take a moment to look at both sides of this issue, as well as study what the Word has to say about investing in our ministries. Let us concentrate on four major areas of investment that affect our ministries: **TIME, TALENT, COMMITMENT,** and **FINANCES**.

TIME: As dancers, we must spend time investing in our ministries. This includes prayer

15

time spent during and outside of scheduled rehearsals. Each dancer must have a prayer life. This can be developed by encouraging regular times of prayer at rehearsal and inviting various team members to pray before and after rehearsals. This allows leaders to note where any individual strengths are and allows for a coaching opportunity regarding effective prayer. If there is a strong team of those willing to be committed to praying for the ministry on a regular basis, an additional prayer team can be established to intercede for the ministry on a regular basis.

We must also invest time in studying the Scriptures. Not only must dancers be aware of what the Bible says concerning dance, but a general understanding of the Word will greatly assist in the correct interpretation of effective choreography, garments, praise, worship, and appropriate conduct in the ministry. Let us make sure that each dancer owns a Bible. We should also encourage them to carry it with them to church services and Bible studies for training and participation.

Much of the time investment is spent in rehearsals and in church. Several hours per week may be spent away from family, friends, and personal responsibilities. As much as possible, our rehearsal times should be consistent, reasonable, and respectful. When we begin rehearsals late, we lose valuable time that could have been used for instruction and development. If we continue to keep ministry members beyond the set time that we are scheduled, resentment and decreased morale may result.

Performing a regular assessment of the use of our time will let us know if the rehearsal time should be extended or shortened, if we must shift to multiple days, or if the timeframe needs to be adjusted to accommodate as many people as possible. Do not expect there to be a perfect schedule to accommodate everyone that is interested. Whatever agreement is set should be done with consideration and in excellence.

We can also save time when investing in our ministries. Remaining focused during rehearsals limits the number of times that directions or announcements need to be repeated. Each dancer must take personal responsibility by becoming aware of his or her placement and positioning during choreography and while listening for cues. There should be no excessive talking or distractions during ministry gatherings. Leaders should develop an orderly system for the asking and answering of questions, addressing concerns, and unity during listening periods. Disrespectful visitors, unwelcomed commentary by guests, and unsupervised children can all be distracting during rehearsal times. We should try to avoid this as much as possible by inviting guests to wait in a separate area, discouraging outside interference, and encouraging parents or guardians to monitor children at all times.

Another way to expedite the time is for all ministry members to familiarize themselves with the song lyrics, supplemental reading materials, and upcoming calendar dates. Developing a solid communication system will allow for organized dissemination of ministry information and the ability to answer any related questions. Leaders or administrators can type song lyrics, create calendars, and give instructions via email, social networking groups, and other technology tools. This can cut down on the use of office supplies and allows ministry members to access the needed documents to print at a more convenient time. As a benefit, the ministry may save dollars by limiting the need for additional printing.

Ministry members must be encouraged to rehearse on their own time so that group gatherings may be used to move forward instead of re-teaching previously shared choreography or materials. There can also be additional time allotted before or after rehearsals for ministry members to receive additional help or extra assistance. Personal responsibility should be taken by each ministry member for the benefit of the whole group.

TALENT: The second area of investment that we must take a look at is how to properly use our God-given talents. Talent is defined as a special, often creative or artistic aptitude or a person of talent or a group of persons of talent in a field or activity. Matthew 25:15-29 contains the Parable of the Talents and outlines the importance of multiplying what has been placed in our hands. The Giver of our talents is expecting a return on investment. Hiding our talents is considered wicked and slothful, and is rooted in fear.

As dancers, we must SPEND or give our talents in the ministry of movement. This includes developing them to become greater. We can accomplish this in several ways. Seeking Godly mentorship, instruction, and information regarding how to enhance our function will help us to multiply in this area. Enrolling in training programs and educational institutes may cost money. We must be willing to invest in instruction for our development.

We can also improve our choreographic abilities and creativity by enrolling in dance classes and attending instructional camps and conferences. While we can learn in any situation, we must prayerfully select instructors and environments that will help us grow without compromising our belief in God. Every dance style may not be readily adaptable for every type of ministry. We must apply lessons learned with wisdom concerning how and if it should be used in our ministry.

We should also obtain an understanding of the basic elements of dance and the ministry of movement by learning terminology, reading books, purchasing DVDs, attending theatrical productions, and researching reliable written materials and the internet.

As we invest in our ministries, we SAVE our talents by guarding against corruption, abuse, arguments, mistreatment, ungodliness, discord, and rebellion within the ministry. We should also refrain from participating in activities that may send a double message in ministry. For example, dancing in a nightclub to learn or exhibit the latest steps on Saturday may not serve as a good witness for Sunday morning ministry from the same dancer.

Living lifestyles laden with sin will also limit us in using our talents over time. Don't think so? Think about the many professed Christians and athletes caught in major scandals and the damage it caused to their careers, families and ministries. Even the "world" expects its leaders to live up to a standard of integrity.

We must also refrain from the temptation to dance for money. If we only allow ourselves to accept invitations based on paychecks, we could very well open the door for us to begin to prostitute the ministry of movement for our own gain. All that we do must be to God's glory! We do not want to develop reputations that we are money-hungry or motivated by profits. We can reference many people in ministry who have fallen victim to greed.

COMMITMENT: A commitment is making an agreement or pledge to do something in the future. Dancers can uphold commitment by maintaining integrity and trust. We must allow ourselves no excuses when it comes to obeying God. We should continue to be faithful and dependable to our leaders, fellow dance ministers, and church families by keeping our promises and honoring our word. When we frequently miss rehearsals, outings, and other scheduled gatherings, we will be viewed as uncommitted. We can avoid being labeled in this way by not agreeing to do more than our time will allow. Too many conflicting activities will hinder our ability to stay committed, even if our intentions were to get the job done.

MONEY: Yes, you read that right! We must invest our money in the ministry. Even the Bible tells us that our treasure is connected to our hearts in Matthew 6:21 *"For where your treasure is, there your heart will be also."* If we are unwilling to use our own funds to develop or grow the ministry, then we must submit ourselves to a heart check-up. Balance must be exercised when it comes to our finances. We should not spend money in ministry (outside of biblical giving) to the detriment of our households and personal responsibilities. Dance ministry participation is not a requirement! Maintaining the local church and supporting the spreading of the Gospel must stay in its proper place as a priority.

Dancers will most likely SPEND money by purchasing garments for ministering in public. It also costs money to maintain these garments by dry cleaning, washing, and repairing them. Often, money is spent on workshops and other trainings. Although this may be a personal expense, some churches will absorb some of these costs, while other ministries are allowed to raise funds to meet these financial goals.

In this image-driven society, many dancers also spend money by paying for professional photos to be used on websites, ministry materials, and other media. Books, DVDs and supplemental materials can be purchased by individuals or by a group. Ministry business cards that are professionally designed also require a budget. Website maintenance, business telephone lines, music purchases and other miscellaneous bills can all impact the bottom line of a ministry. This statement is true: Ministry comes with a price!

We can operate as good stewards when we research ways to SAVE money to stretch our budgets. Planning in advance usually saves significant money when registering for events, planning to travel, purchasing new garments, or preparing for ministry dates. For many churches, the budget is set in advance for each ministry. Understanding this number and maximizing dollar value will benefit us instead of hinder us.

We will not properly understand how to use ministry finances unless we understand our priorities. What is needed first? What will provide the most benefit to all parties involved? What can be donated to us instead of purchased? We should research to see where we can get the best price on items that are widely available. If the members in a ministry have limited funds, purchasing a solid color base garment and using various overlays may stretch the dollar further. One garment purchased once every few years will eventually become outdated as we age or experience changes in our bodies.

We should also seek to sow into other ministries to be a blessing. We should prepare an offering to bring when we come into the house of the Lord. Often during services and concerts, dancers forget to carry money on their person when we are concerned with our garments, choreography, seating, etc. We can carry a small container or wallet to be used during times of ministry to hold money, keys, or other small necessities.

We can also support fellow ministries in other ways. Showing up to dance programs when we are not scheduled to minister can be a great show of support to our fellow dance ministers. We can offer words of encouragement to other ministries as they move forward in their area of ministry as God leads us. Giving out compliments purely for flattery and not from the spirit of truth reeks of wrong motives.

If we SPEND time obeying God in the areas He has called us to serve, lives will be SAVED as the message goes forth. The name JESUS or Yeshua means "Salvation" "Jehovah Saves," or "The One Who Saves." Hosanna comes from a Hebrew phrase meaning "Save, O God." Hosanna in the Highest would mean "Save us in the highest way." When we lift up Jesus, He does the drawing. Being good stewards over our ministries whether we SPEND or SAVE will assist us in lifting Him up for many generations to come to Christ.

CAUSE 4

WORSHIP, INC.

In my time of ministering through dance, I have been, more often than not, the spectator in the waiting. Whether ministering during a dance concert, church service, or special occasion, there is a time to stand back and observe. Have I experienced frustration? Yes. Boredom? Yes. Impatience? Yes. I have also experienced overwhelming joy, thankfulness, and the desire to break out into spontaneous celebration. What is it that makes others seek to worship Him along with the dancer?

I agree that some dance presentations resemble a performance more than a ministry. Some ministries have been classified "angels" on the platform and deemed "divas" offstage. It is often a challenge to get up and "minister" in an atmosphere that has been saturated with entertainment.

It is at these times that I feel the most vulnerable. There is the mounting pressure to "set the atmosphere," "tear down strongholds," and "usher in the Presence of the Lord." Several times after ministering before people, I have been approached by many who said that they "didn't know how to respond to what they felt on the inside." I do not believe that this is

God's intended design for public worship.

As a movement minister, I realize that I am not merely a spectacle for others to sit back and critique. For corporate worship to occur as a result of my dance ministry presentation, I realize that my true responsibility is that of Praise & Worship "Usher." In understanding my position as a dance minister, I agree with Michael & Vivien Hibbert's statement in the article *Expressing the Moods of the Holy Spirit*:

> "The ultimate in worship is not the expression of worship, but the knowledge of His presence. It is not the music or the songs of the Lord or the dance – these expressions must come out of knowing Him- they must be a result of worship rather than being acts of worship."

Worship Defined

I have unfortunately realized that the accepted definition of worship today, at times, is viewed as a one-person or small group activity (i.e. the rise of 'Superstar' Praise & Worship Leaders and the explosion of Praise & Worship teams in most churches). Upon studying the Scriptures regarding worship, I found many instances of Worship, Incorporated. This is how Merriam-Webster defines **incorporate**:

1) To unite or work into something already existent so as to form an indistinguishable whole: to blend or combine thoroughly

2) To form into a legal corporation: To admit to membership in a corporate body

3) To give material form to: EMBODY.

We find one of several Old Testament examples of corporate worship in 2 Chronicles 28:29,

> *"So all the assembly worshiped, the singers sang, and the trumpeters sounded; all this continued until the burnt offering was finished."*

The Hebrew defines the word <u>all</u> as **kol** (#3605) meaning all, any, every, what (where, who) - soever, (the) whole. I do not see children, the elderly, or the lame excluded from this worship assembly.

For further instructions concerning New Testament worship, we see a few Greek words that point to the Lord's desire for a unified body in worship: **Episunagoge** (#1997) from #1996; meaning, a complete collection; especially a Christian meeting (for worship): assembling (gathering) together. We also see this in **sumphoneo** (#4856); meaning to be harmonious, to accord or stipulate: agree (together, with). Sumphoneo is akin to the word symphony. A symphony consists of many different instruments, but they all play the same song, in the same key, in time together, to be complete. I am reminded as a dancer and movement minister to be careful not to think that the dance is the most important component being used to impact the worship experience. It is indeed an awesome sight when all aspects of worship including instruments, singing, and movement function together to produce Worship, Incorporated.

The Incorporation Process

There are several passages of Scripture that highlight the importance of Worship, Incorporated. Let's take a look at 2 Chronicles 29:27-29 (NKJV):

> *"Then Hezekiah commanded* them *to offer the burnt offering on the altar. And when the burnt offering began, the song of the LORD also began, with the trumpets and with the instruments of David king of Israel. So all the assembly worshiped, the singers sang, and the trumpeters sounded; all this continued until the burnt offering was finished. And when they had finished offering, the king and all who were present with him bowed and worshiped."*

Though the Lord has gifted many with dance, we must also remember that dance ministry is not assigned to everyone, but movement (bowing) in this example was done by the entire assembly!

Yet another Scripture points to the power of corporate unity:

"And Ezra blessed the LORD, the great God. Then all the people answered, 'Amen, Amen!' while lifting up their hands. And they bowed their heads and worshiped the LORD with their faces to the ground." - Nehemiah 8:6

We see here again, that all the people lifted their hands and bowed (that's movement) corporately. The people did not excuse themselves based on personal feelings or preferences. Just to make sure that we understand how powerful corporate worship is, 2 Chronicles 7:3 informs us,

"When all the children of Israel saw how the fire came down, and the glory of the LORD on the temple, they bowed their faces to the ground on the pavement, and worshiped and praised the LORD, saying: "For He is good, For His mercy endures forever."

Unity is essential to the corporate worship establishment!

The Present Worship Report

We often use Scripture to talk about worship in spirit and in truth. Though the Bible accounts for us many instances of Worship, Incorporated, it seems as though many factions of the worship department have broken off into their own "companies." Choirs, praise teams, musicians, dancers, and ministers of the Word often decide separately what the most important area of concentration should be, while ignoring the larger corporate umbrella of congregational worship. Competition inevitably arises as to which unit is the most responsible for leading the congregation into a worship experience.

More and more, I am witnessing Pastors, musicians, singers, and dancers participating together in corporate praise and worship in major congregations (and smaller ones too!). A return to the biblical model has begun: NOW IS THE TIME!

Future Worship Projections

Not only was this a pattern for the past, we are informed that future worship shall also be Worship, Incorporated. The Bible gives several glimpses into the future worship portal: *"All the ends of the world shall remember and turn to the LORD, and all the families of the nations shall worship before You."* -Psalm 22:27

It is wonderful to see that neither denomination, race, nor geography will hinder the future of Worship, Incorporated as prophesied in Revelation 15:4, *"Who shall not fear You, O Lord, and glorify Your name? For You alone are holy. For all nations shall come and worship before You, for Your judgments have been manifested."*

Not only will this happen in the earth realm, but in the heavenly kingdom also: *"All the angels stood around the throne and the elders and the four living creatures, and fell on their faces before the throne and worshiped God."* -Revelation 7:11

The Bottom Line: Business Matters

Worship, Incorporated must lead to a return on the investment that our Heavenly Father has placed in us. Although He created each one of us uniquely and with great care, He orchestrated it in such a way that we as many members fit together. He has designed us to succeed and has plans to prosper us. We must realize that each of us is essential to the success of Worship, Incorporated. Like Jesus in Luke 2:49, we must be also about our Father's business, and that is to have pleasant unity among the many members of His Body.

WORSHIP, INC.

Sources
http://www.eliyah.com/lexicon.html (Hebrew and Greek Word definitions)

Make His Praise Glorious Manual (119)

CAUSE 5

If the Shoe Fits...

"If the shoe fits, wear it!" An often used quote, but does it always apply to dance ministers? In the Walt Disney fairy tale of *Cinderella,* her glass slipper was lost after a dance celebration in the kingdom. The slipper was depicted as clear in color, and a unique fit for the wearer. Several tried on the shoe in an attempt to impersonate Cinderella as the prince searched the population for his once-upon-a-time dance companion, but it did not "fit" them, and they were left undiscovered.

I received an e-mail once regarding difficulty in choosing a song to minister to that matched a particular theme. There are many traditional church events occurring throughout the year that usually have a pre-selected theme: Concerts, Community Events, Church Anniversary, Dedication Services, Pastor and Wife's Anniversary, Pastor's Appreciation, Women's Day, Men's Day, Usher's Day, Youth Day, Conferences... (Shall I continue?). Relating to my own experience in trying to "match" a theme, it's often tough to "make it fit" while maintaining the authenticity of the ministry God has entrusted me with.

When selecting songs for ministry, it can become frustrating at times when we cannot find exactly what we think will fit the theme. Sometimes that is good because God wants us to be open. We should consider songs that may deal with the overall message of the theme or occasion, even if the specific words are not a perfect match. Sometimes we can unite a song with a theme by explaining the piece before we dance and how it relates to the occasion or idea.

The first priority is to seek the Lord for guidance when selecting songs. In my years as a dance minister, I have often found that even when I was unaware of a theme in advance, the song that was selected often matched with the flow of the service. For example, during one service in which we were invited to minister, the phrase "Thank You, Lord" was said repeatedly over the pulpit by the guests and the keynote speaker. We were overjoyed because we had already selected a song entitled "Thank You," to dance to! Although "Thank You" was not the official theme of the service, per se, it flowed with the Spirit and promoted unity during the gathering.

The song has to minister to **you** first. Explain it if you have to, but don't ever feel that you are forced to choose a song that seems to "fit" perfectly. What is speaking to your spirit right **now**, even if it does not seem to match the theme exactly? When studying the

Scriptures, you might just be surprised at what the Lord reveals. I love how God works! He compels us to diligently and earnestly seek Him.

Even if the proverbial "shoe" fits and is just the right size for us, it may not be appropriate for a particular occasion. We cannot wear tennis shoes on the ice skating rink. Some songs work for some occasions, but not for others. We do not want to wear shoes that do not fit in ministry. We will either get stuck, injured, or be embarrassed when missteps occur. It's good to strive to be appropriate, decent and orderly for every gathering that we are assigned to minister in the context of true worship.

Be sensitive to the leading of the Lord and trust Him when He speaks to you about a particular song. For those who are in dance ministries and may not have a vote in what songs are selected for the ministry, pray for the Lord to lead those who do to select songs that fit the mission of the group.

There also comes a time when the season or style changes and it's time to stop ministering certain selections. Sandals in the winter will not work for obvious reasons. We must also know when the season for a particular song has come to an end, or is no longer speaking to the ministry as a whole. As ministries continue to grow in the knowledge and understanding of the Lord and His Word, there may be a maturing that affects the types of songs that the ministry will embrace.

Thank Him for the moments that you are compelled to keep searching for the "right" song to dance to, even when you feel exasperated. Often when I am ready to stop listening to music for new choreography, God reveals to me that I have already heard the song before. He opens my ears to hear it when the time is right for me to minister it with power and conviction. When I listen to His voice and obey His leading, it always "fits."

CAUSE 6

When a Standard-Bearer Fainteth

Isaiah 10:15-18 (KJV)

Shall the axe boast itself against him that heweth therewith? Or shall the saw magnify itself against him that shaketh it? As if the rod should shake itself against them that lift it up, or as if the staff should lift up itself, as if it were no wood.

Therefore shall the Lord, the Lord of hosts, send among his fat ones leanness; and under his glory he shall kindle a burning like the burning of a fire.

And the light of Israel shall be for a fire, and his Holy One for a flame: and it shall burn and devour his thorns and his briers in one day;

And shall consume the glory of his forest, and of his fruitful field, both soul and body: and they shall be as when a standard-bearer fainteth.

This passage refers to Sennacherib, King of Assyria who was covetous, ambitious, and bragged about his own power. Those who are very talented and celebrated in the worship arts arena must constantly resist the temptation to glory in the gift. We must strive to give honor to God, or we may find ourselves fainting instead of standing in Him.

The Hebrew word for faint used here is **macac** (H4549) meaning to faint (with fatigue, fear or grief), discourage, melt away. Standard-Bearer is a Greek word, **hupodeiknumi**, meaning to exhibit under the eyes, to show by placing under the eyes (DANCE!), to show by words and argument, to teach (DANCE!). It also means to forewarn, or to show by making known future things (PROPHETIC DANCE!).

Historically, a standard was an ensign or flag that would be lifted up above the camp to the tribes of Israel that clarified identifications. A standard was also a banner that was set upon a high mountain in the case of an invasion that indicated to the people the place that they were to assemble. It is also a column or lofty pole, or a sign by which one is warned.

A standard-bearer was a person who carried a standard, especially of a military unit. He was also a leader or representative of a movement, organization or political party, an officer or a military unit who bears a standard. It could also be any person, military or civilian, who bears an emblem which is used as a visual symbol.

In ancient Rome, troops would go to battle with a standard-bearer. This person would be a brave soldier who would drape himself with animal skin (like lion or bear) over his helmet and down his back. He would stand in a prominent place on the battlefield. On the end of his pole would be the ensign or standard, which was often an eagle, or the face or head of the ruling emperor to remind the troops for whom they were fighting. When we raise the standard, it serves as a reminder and indicator of Who we represent!

Let us look at several important factors about the standard:

The standard is a sign of loyalty.

Jeremiah 4:6 (King James Version)

Set up the standard toward Zion: retire, stay not: for I will bring evil from the north, and a great destruction.

The standard would indicate the progress of the battle.

Isaiah 62:10 (King James Version)

Go through, go through the gates; prepare ye the way of the people; cast up, cast up the highway; gather out the stones; lift up a standard for the people.

The standard was the way order was maintained in the battle.

In Rome, a cornicen or horn-blower would dress in animal skin and sound the trumpet for two reasons:

1) To cause others to look at the standard and to get in the right position.

2) To give out commands from the officers to keep order in the battle.

If the standard-bearer was killed or ran away, the entire unit would go into a panic and end up in disarray. This signals defeat and disbands the group. In many dance and movement ministries, the "standard-bearer" would be considered the leader of a group, or those who stand out front in a group. I often remind all dancers that when we stand in front of people we are all leaders by default, with or without a title in front of our names.

The standard-bearer served as both an occasional position of service (like during a parade) or a permanent position (on the battlefield). Because others could see the standard lifted up above them, it was used as a form of communication for the group and promoted unity in the ranks. They were used in religious rituals, contained precious metals and exhibited detailed craftsmanship. Losing the standard was considered to be a disgrace.

Even if we are not carrying flags and banners in our hands, our garments can also stand as symbols of service or loyalty to our Commander (God). Psalm 60:4 declares, *"Thou hast given a banner to them that fear thee, that it may be displayed because of the truth. Selah."*

Other words for standard are **ensign**, which is a flag of a military ship or unit which served as items of identification (banners, badges, and signal flags) and **flag**, which is a piece of fabric flown from a pole or mast used as an identifier. Flags are most commonly used to identify countries. A **banner** is a flag or cloth bearing a symbol, slogan, logo, or message. Banners were also used to rally troops and declare allegiance. The word banner comes from the Latin word bandum (flag cloth), which is derived from the word banns (meaning official proclamation). Abandon means to change loyalty or disobey orders and means "to leave the cloth or flag!"

Ministers in churches are often referred to as "men of the cloth." This would mean that when a standard-bearer refuses to be faithful to this position, it would be symbolic of leaving the faith! To serve as a standard-bearer comes with a high level of both spiritual and personal responsibility. Jesus Himself became both a banner and a standard-bearer during the crucifixion. In John 12:32 (KJV) He says, *"And I, if I be lifted up from the earth, will draw all men unto me."*

What does this have to do with the dance ministry? We serve as standard-bearers when we stand in front of the congregation, when we wear garments with fabric and symbols, as we carry flags, when we display banners, as we utilize streamers during processionals, and in our daily lives. What causes us to faint as standard-bearers in ministry and how can we avoid causing confusion and miscommunication in ministry?

PRIDE

Daniel 5:20 (KJV)

But when his heart was lifted up, and his mind hardened in pride, he was deposed from his kingly throne, and they took his glory from him.

Pride will cause us to lose our footing as standard-bearers. We are often warned that pride goes before destruction! Selfish pride will destroy arts ministries very rapidly. We must continue to remain humble, teachable, and submitted if we desire to abide in our God-appointed position.

LACK OF KNOWLEDGE

Amos 8:12-14 (KJV)

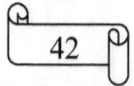

And they shall wander from sea to sea, and from the north even to the east, they shall run to and fro to seek the word of the LORD, and shall not find it.

In that day shall the fair virgins and young men faint for thirst.

They that swear by the sin of Samaria, and say, Thy god, O Dan, liveth; and, the manner of Beersheba liveth; even they shall fall, and never rise up again.

We perish for lack of knowledge. Many dance ministries that are unable to sustain longevity suffer being dismantled because of a lack of applying and living by the Word of God. Ministries that are built on personalities instead of establishing Christ as the foundation will not endure.

We must make sure to know the Word of the Lord for ourselves so that we will not have to look for it to come through others. Those who belong to Him are able to recognize and follow His voice. When we know something, we are required to be accountable for that which we have been made aware. It is time to live the life that we dance about. We must become doers of the Word more than doers of the dance.

DISOBEDIENCE (SIN)

Jonah 2:7 (KJV)
When my soul fainted within me I remembered the LORD: and my prayer came in unto thee, into thine holy temple.

Psalm 31:10 (KJV)

For my life is spent with grief, and my years with sighing: my strength faileth because of mine iniquity, and my bones are consumed.

Without a doubt, sin will cause us to become disqualified in ministry. Not only will we limit our ability to reach others, we can also become laden with the guilt that often accompanies it. Sin prevents us from moving forward with confidence after the breach has occurred. Although we may still have a gift in ministry, once sins are discovered, ungodly lifestyles and habits will diminish the extent of our reach and impair our influence.

Sin that is practiced in the lives of leaders will scatter the group and also opens the door for hurt and distrust to grow like a wildfire. Disregard for the Lord's commandments among ministry members will compromise the overall reputation of the ministry and encourage offenses to develop within the team and throughout a congregation. Praise God for His grace and mercy, but we must remember that sin pays wages that result in death!

EXPOSURE

Jonah 4:8 (King James Version)
And it came to pass, when the sun did arise, that God prepared a vehement east wind; and the sun beat upon the head of Jonah, that he fainted, and wished in himself to die, and said, It is better for me to die than to live.

When we allow prolonged sin and disobedience to frame our character, we will allow our private failures to become public information. The more popular we may become in ministry, the more damaging negative exposure can be for our ministries. Covering up our missteps is not a remedy for lack of integrity or poor character. Immediate repentance and refusal to fall into iniquity will provide the grace needed to escape infamy. Even if we allow ourselves to be caught in a net, the Lord is able to deliver us when our hearts are right with Him.

JESUS is the STANDARD!

Isaiah 11:10-12 (King James Version)
And in that day there shall be a root of Jesse, which shall stand for an ensign of the people; to it shall the Gentiles seek: and his rest shall be glorious.

And it shall come to pass in that day, that the Lord shall set his hand again the second time to recover the remnant of his people, which shall be left, from Assyria, and from Egypt, and from

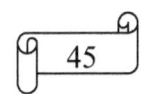

Pathros, and from Cush, and from Elam, and from Shinar, and from Hamath, and from the islands of the sea.

And he shall set up an ensign for the nations, and shall assemble the outcasts of Israel, and gather together the dispersed of Judah from the four corners of the earth.

We must be committed to following Christ completely. Jesus Himself became the living standard and is the standard-bearer that never faints. When we lift Him up in our lives and before others, He will do the drawing. We can only continue to uphold the standard when we lift Christ above all else in our lives.

If there are any areas in which we have let the standard down, we must again regain the strength and endurance to carry our cross on a daily basis. Through Jesus, we will be able to do those things which strengthen us. Without Him, it will be impossible to hold the standard high when we allow the flesh to lead the way.

CAUSE 7

A Song and Dance

The Song of Moses

For Moses, it all started with a song...

> *"Then sang Moses and the children of Israel this song unto the LORD, and spake, saying, I will sing unto the LORD, for He hath triumphed gloriously: the horse and his rider hath He thrown into the sea. The LORD is my strength and song, and He is become my salvation: He is my God, and I will prepare Him an habitation; my father's God, and I will exalt Him."* -Exodus 15:1-2

This marked the beginning of a new era in the lives of the children of Israel after the crossing of the Red Sea. In response, we see a first in the Bible, as Miriam takes a timbrel in her hand and leads the women in dance (Exodus 15:20).

A totally new visual display of the plan of the Lord was revealed to Moses out of his intimate relationship with God. Moses was given precise instructions on how to prepare a place for the Lord to dwell among His people. He was instructed to build a tabernacle or tent for the Lord's dwelling in Exodus 25:8-9, *"And let them make Me a sanctuary; that I may dwell among them. According to all that I shew thee, after the pattern of the tabernacle, and the pattern of all the instruments thereof, even so shall ye make it."*

The meaning of the word tabernacle in the Hebrew here is **mishkan** (Strong's #4908) meaning: a residence (including a shepherd's hut, the lair of animals, figuratively, the grave; also the Temple); specifically, the Tabernacle (properly, its wooden walls):--dwelleth, dwelling (place), habitation, tabernacle, tent. Another Hebrew word is also used to describe this dwelling in Exodus 26:9, *"And thou shalt couple five curtains by themselves, and six curtains by themselves, and shalt double the sixth curtain in the forefront of the tabernacle."* The word for tabernacle used here is **'ohel** (Strong's 168): a tent (as clearly conspicuous from a distance):--covering, (dwelling)(place), home, tabernacle, tent. The Lord was definitely up to something here, as we will see upon our continued look at the tabernacles.

Dancing David

A dance ushered in a new era of worship for David and his people. David realized that the Ark of the Covenant belonged with Israel. David took action by preparing a place for it beforehand: *"And David made him houses in the city of David, and prepared a place for the ark of God, and pitched for it a tent."* (1 Chronicles 15:1)   David then assembled Israel together, leading the procession of the ark: *"Thus all Israel brought up the ark of the covenant of the LORD with shouting, and with sound of the cornet, and with trumpets, and with cymbals, making a noise with psalteries and harps. And it came to pass, as the ark of the covenant of the LORD came to the city of David, that Michal, the daughter of Saul looking out at a window saw king David dancing and playing: and she despised him in her heart."* (1 Chronicles 15:28-29)

The tent that David pitched is defined **'ohel**, but not **mishkan**.   There were distinct differences between the Tabernacle of Moses and the Tabernacle of David.   The detailing of all of this would fill volumes if I highlighted each and every difference.   I will attempt to discuss the main message from the comparison of the two.

Settling the Differences

The results are very clear: Moses had his work cut out for him!   The Tabernacle of Moses was very detailed and required the involvement of many people.   In the book of Exodus, we read the details given to Moses by the Lord that had to be constructed according to the exact pattern shown to Moses.   Moses was as God to the people, and the priests were ordained to minister to their needs. For David, we simply see that he prepared a place (tent) for the Ark of the Covenant. Missing from David's account are any detailed instructions as to how this tent was to be erected. As king, he is also seen performing priestly duties concerning the affairs of God. Thus begins to unfold a new dimension in the relationship between the Lord and His people.

Furnishings in Moses' tabernacle were symbolic in nature and included the Ark of the Covenant, Table of Shewbread, Golden Candlestick, Altar of Incense, Brasen Altar, and the Brasen Laver. These were constructed by Master Craftsmen who were filled with wisdom to carry out the tasks precisely. This furniture was placed within the tabernacle. The outer court contained the Brasen Altar representing sacrifice and atonement and the Brasen Laver, which symbolized washing and cleansing. The Holy Place housed the Golden Candlestick (light/illumination and oil for the Spirit), the Table of Shewbread (12 loaves/12 tribes- Bread of Life), and the Altar of Incense (prayer). A veil divided the Holy Place from the Most Holy Place. Behind this divide dwelt the Ark of the Covenant (the Presence of the Lord).

David was described as a man after God's own heart. It is no surprise that the only piece of furniture David placed in the tent was the Ark of the Covenant, for he desired the Lord's presence in his life above all else! The Ark was placed in the center of the tent, making the presence of the Lord the focus of worship in David's Tabernacle. This shift signifies the value of worship over sacrifice and is an integral symbol of the priority of Divine relationship. There was no veil barring access in David's tabernacle! It was open and accessible.

There was a noted difference regarding the contents of the Ark between Moses and David. In David's Ark, both the manna and Aaron's rod were missing. What happened to them is not detailed. We do know that the manna and the rod were a part of the wilderness experience. After being led by Moses for many years, the children of Israel entered the promised land! No more wandering, no more guessing.

Access restrictions also greatly changed. In the era of Moses, the priest entered the Holy of Holies only once per year on the Day of Atonement. For David, the presence of the Lord was a daily requirement and priests were appointed by David to minister before the Lord continually with musical instruments.

Moses was an appointed leader. David was an anointed leader. Why is this significant? In the times of the Pharoahs, rulership was determined by birth into the dynasty. Moses, though not born into the house of Pharoah, was

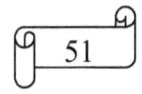

adopted and raised in his house, like a son. He knew the ways of the Egyptians as well as the inner workings of the house of Pharaoh, and this gave him access to the throne, facilitating the exodus of the children of Israel. David, on the other hand, was just a shepherd boy. He did not come from the lineage of kings. He was chosen by God, and anointed for kingship. This gives hope to any person today. God anoints His people without regard to heritage, for He is no respecter of persons. He can use anyone for His service.

The Same Yesterday, Today and Forevermore

Though there were many differences between the two tabernacles, there were also some noteworthy similarities. The main focus of the two tabernacles was the Ark of the Covenant. The Ark first appeared at Moses' tabernacle and he was given the exact pattern regarding its construction. Made of shittim wood and overlaid with gold within and without, it was designed to be transported on staves and included a mercy seat with cherubim atop. Here is where the Lord communed with Moses, and the Ark became a symbol for His presence. David's desire was to return the Ark to its rightful place: with the people of the Lord.

Inside the Ark were found the Tables of Testimony. These were the commandments given by God to Moses on Mount Sinai. The Lord's covenant with His people was outlined with the finger of God. They were instructed to keep His commandments. Though the manna and Aaron's rod were missing by the time David secured it, this one thing remained the same: His law was not to depart from the Children of Israel. His covenant with them is everlasting.

Both of the tents had coverings or curtains draped over them (Exodus 26:1, 1 Chronicles 17:1). This was necessary to be maintained as a symbol of the Lord's covering regarding these two leaders and the continued favor regarding children of Israel. This covering also served as a protection for the tabernacles.

The holiness of God is highlighted for both Moses and David. An unclean priest entering into the Holy of Holies resulted in sudden death. When Uzza put his hand on the Ark of the Covenant, he was immediately smitten and died on the spot (1 Chronicles 13:9). The presence of the Lord and the Holy things of God are not to be taken lightly. We see in these examples that the Lord must be consulted about the proper order concerning His ordinances.

Levitical involvement was crucial for both Moses and David. The Levitical priesthood was established by the Lord at the time of Moses and resulted in the appointment of Aaron and his sons as ministering priests ordained for tabernacle service (1 Chronicles 6:49). David appointed Levites to minister before the Ark of the Lord (1 Chronicles 16:37). Levites also were appointed to transport the holy things of the Lord. The ordination of priests for service in the house of the Lord was maintained, making servanthood a necessary part of tabernacle worship.

Both Moses and David were leaders chosen by God to lead the Children of Israel into relationship with Him. These men were both favored by the Lord Himself, and gave instruction to the people as to how the Lord's tabernacle was to be established. The Lord continues to use leaders today to lead people into His presence.

Something Old, Something New

The patterns of the tabernacles are still significant for the church today. As the Ark was taken by the enemy and was later recovered by David, we often hear the history of how the worship arts were taken by the enemy, but are now being restored. The battle lines between the "traditional" church vs. the contemporary church have become evident in the evolution of music and the increase of worship arts ministries in many churches of today.

Many churches have chosen to follow the Moses model: Sticking to the exact pattern of by-laws and protocol established many years ago. Other churches have gone the way of David: Placing the presence of the Lord at the center of worship services, with freedom of worship expression encouraged and embraced. The debate rages on, as many people have rejected the customs of old for a fresh type of faith. As we saw in the case of Uzza, the Lord is still Holy and must be revered as such. It is important for the church to move into a new level of intimacy with God without forsaking His holiness. The church as a whole must continue to seek the Lord concerning how He would have us to proceed as He brings about a restoration of David's tabernacle.

We should find no awe in how the worship arts are coming to the forefront. His word prophesies in Acts 15:16-17, *"After this I will return, and will build again the tabernacle of David, which is fallen down; and I will build again the ruins thereof, and I will set it up: That the residue of men might seek after the Lord, and all the Gentiles, upon whom my name is called, saith the Lord, who doeth all these things."* The Greek word used for "fallen down" here is **pipto** (Strong's #4098) meaning: to fall from a state of uprightness, disappear, cease, lose authority, no longer have force, to fail of participating in, miss a share in. As the understanding of the worship arts is being enhanced through many conferences, books, websites, and from many pulpits today, the power of true worship is gaining ground and changing lives forever.

We are witnessing how praise and worship units are becoming essential in many worship services worldwide. Dance ministries are being incorporated during live music recordings, filming in movies, and appearing on television and other media outlets. As worship artists continue to seek the Lord and increase the understanding of God's intent for worship, many more doors will continue to be opened for others to be birthed into a more intimate relationship with God. The restoration is upon us, however; we must be careful not to mishandle His presence as Uzza did. *Holiness becometh thine house, oh Lord, for ever...* (Psalm 93:5).

Open the Eyes of My Heart, Lord...

The eyes of our understanding open as we spend more time in His presence. As the Levites carried the burden of the Lord's presence on their shoulders, worshipping artists must too understand the importance of how we carry Him with us wherever we go. We must grasp the truth that His presence is portable, and not confined to any one region. The earth is the Lord's! We can now enter His presence boldly through Jesus (Heb 10:9).

We are entering into a time in which worship in no longer being considered a one-size-fits-all model. Singers, musicians, dancers, ministers, preachers, servants, and congregants are coming into the knowledge of how the Body of Christ is jointly fit together. There is a place for all of the children of the Lord in the order of worship, because we now know that WE are His tabernacle. His tent of dwelling in within us, and He inhabits our praises (Psalm 22:3).

The former tabernacles were a foreshadowing of what was to come in the form of our Lord Jesus Christ. This is confirmed in Hebrews 10:20-25 which reads, *"By a new and living way* (not of dead animal sacrifice as in Moses' Tabernacle, but by Jesus Christ), *which He hath consecrated for us* (set apart as the Levites were sanctified), *through the veil* (place of separation in Tabernacle of Moses, rent by the tearing of the flesh [veil] of Jesus), *that is to say, his flesh* (the ultimate sacrifice and triumph over sin for which animals could not atone); *And having an high priest over the house of God* (Levitical Priesthood for Tabernacles. Now Christ Jesus as King-Priest); *Let us draw near* (direct access to God with boldness; no longer residing in the outer court) *with a true heart in full assurance of faith, having our hearts sprinkled* (blood sprinkled in Moses' Tabernacle from external source. The sprinkling of our hearts being an internal, personal experience) *from an evil conscience* (sin), *and our bodies washed with pure water* (Bronze Laver was used for washing. Now the washing is by the Word). *Let us hold fast the profession of our faith without wavering* (impossible to please the Lord without faith); *for he is faithful that promised* (covenant keeper*); And let us consider one another to provoke unto love and to good works: Not forsaking the assembling of ourselves together* (Tabernacle of Meeting, now the Body of Christ), *as the manner of some is; but exhorting one another* (Psalms, Hymns, Spiritual Songs)*: and so much the more, as ye see the day approaching* (fulfillment of biblical prophecy)." -Emphasis in parenthesis and interpretation is the author's.

The Tabernacle of David will come to full restoration. We are seeing the elements begin to come together as worship is being restored in our daily lives and in our church gatherings. As we keep the Presence of the Lord and His instruction (Word) close to our hearts, we will witness a return to Glory as has not been witnessed for many generations.

Moses began his assignment with a song; David ushered his in with a dance. Kingdom building plans are given, ordained, and established by the Lord. As we each fulfill the unique assignment that God has given each of us concerning His dwelling in us, we will witness the Glory of the Lord rising as never before!

Sources
http://www.eliyah.com/lexicon.html (Hebrew & Greek)
Make His Praise Glorious Manual (9)
King James Bible Version

CAUSE 8

The Hands Which Hang

Now no chastening seems to be joyful for the present, but painful; nevertheless, afterward it yields the peaceable fruit of righteousness to those who have been trained by it.

Therefore strengthen the hands which hang down, and the feeble knees, and make straight paths for your feet, so that what is lame may not be dislocated, but rather be healed.

D
O
W
N

- Hebrews 12:11-13

In recent church history, the pews have been rocked with scandal after scandal. We witnessed many prominent Christian leaders openly displayed for the public to see and ridicule. Although much publicity surrounded the state of the church, there was much more going on behind the scenes than we could have imagined...

You may not have heard the story of the dance leader who was on the edge of walking away from the ministry. No one may have pulled you to the side and told you that they were dancing while unemployed. That smiling dancer that you saw turning and leaping may have been on the verge of having a nervous breakdown, but there was no front page article or mass media coverage to bring it to the forefront.

There may have been a worshiper that you thought was crying in church because they loved the Lord, but they were really dealing with severe depression. That powerful praise dancer that greeted you in the hallway may have gone home to a husband or other family member who verbally (and maybe even physically) abuses her.

That male dancer may have walked away from a past of affection towards his own gender, and now a church leader is showing up at his residence after-hours to offer "personal counseling sessions." Yes, we are facing a crisis of massive proportions. It's time to walk in the light.

Take a Look at Me Now...

We must be more vigilant than ever concerning the ministries that God gave us. The enemy seeks to destroy our joy, peace, and purpose in the Lord. It is important that we first deal with ourselves before we can deal with anybody else. Are you living a life that is upright before the Lord? Do you spend way too much time talking about the shortcomings of your leader instead of building them up? Are you allowing yourself to indulge in thoughts that you know will lead to acting out the thing which you imagined? Submit yourself to the Lord and allow Him to cleanse you completely and allow Him to perform His sanctification of you entirely.

When Leadership Falters

Are you feeling disappointed in someone that you look to for guidance? Have you been guilty of wanting a particular leader to leave or sit down so that you can finally have your chance to set things straight? It's not easy to deal with a leader who may miss the mark at times, or who may be experiencing a season of transition. Although I do not advocate blindly following someone who is not following Christ, I will say that many leaders fail at the hands of their own flock.

The Hands of Moses

"And so it was, when Moses held up his hand, that Israel prevailed; and when he let down his hand, Amalek prevailed. But Moses' hands became heavy; so they took a stone and put it under him, and he sat on it. And Aaron and Hur supported his hands, one on one side, and the other on the other side; and his hands were steady until the going down of the sun. So Joshua defeated Amalek and his people with the edge of the sword."

- Exodus 17:11-13

THE HANDS WHICH HANG DOWN

Though our leaders bear the responsibility of leading us in the way of the Lord, it is no argument that leadership gets downright tiring at times. It is during these times that trusted co-laborers should make an effort to hold up the hands of the leader. Because Aaron and Hur held up Moses' hands, the entire company of them obtained the victory.

Please hear me! Aaron did not say "Moses, you are really tired, and I think that it is time for you to let someone else lead. I just think that I will take over from here." Unfortunately, too many aspiring leaders take this position instead of assisting the leader. If God selected you to lead, your time will come. It is better to hold up the hands of someone else than to betray them with a knife in the back. Ungodly leadership will be handled on the Lord's terms. We do not have to make an occasion for anyone to be removed by our hands. God will indeed handle it.

> *"Son of man, I have broken the arm of Pharaoh king of Egypt; and see, it has not been bandaged for healing, nor a splint put on to bind it, to make it strong enough to hold a sword. Therefore thus says the Lord GOD: 'Surely I am against Pharaoh king of Egypt, and will break his arms, both the strong one and the one that was broken; and I will make the sword fall out of his hand."* -Ezekiel 30:21-22

Be Strong in the Lord

We must continue to build ourselves and one another up in the Word. Not only must we continue to sharpen our Biblical knowledge, pray, fast, and give, we must also keep our physical bodies strong and healthy. It is written of the virtuous woman in Proverbs 31:17, *"She girds herself with strength, and strengthens her arms."*

When is the last time that you exercised or went to dance class? No one else can do this for us. It is more difficult to minister effectively when we are carrying extra "burdens" or are not getting enough nutrition. Leaders have even more responsibility to care for themselves. If leaders do not take the steps to care for themselves, then it will eventually be impossible for them to provide sufficient care for others.

Lead Me to the Rock

Leaders, be encouraged. There are people who are looking for you to prevail. When you succeed, the people standing with you (and holding up your arms) will be victorious as well. There were times for me personally when I just did not feel like dancing. I showed up anyway and afterward received several testimonies from others about the impact that the ministry had on their lives. What assignment would I have missed if I did not show up that day?

On the other hand, there are also times when leaders must know what assignments to accept, and which to decline. If we train up other leaders who can do mighty exploits for the Kingdom, then everyone will not have to rely on the primary leader to get the job done. Read the Book! Moses was told to appoint people to assist him because he was being "worn out" trying to handle it all by himself!

A Company Keeper

Regardless of our place or service in the ministry, we have a responsibility to strengthen one another. Make it your personal assignment to do something over the next few days to show your leader that he or she is appreciated. Send a card, write a letter, make a phone call, or simply pray. If you have done anything to put a strain on the arms of your leader, confess it, repent and move on. If you are leading (and bleeding) allow the Lord to heal your wounds and rise up and walk. Lives are at stake.

We must also carefully consider the company of those we walk with. If the season for a relationship is ending, it's best to end things on good terms to minimize offense. When we choose to align ourselves with leaders, we must not do so with selfish or impure intentions. When choosing the company we keep, God is the best judge of character that we can rely on to lead us in the right direction.

Forgetting Those Things...

Last season is gone, and it's time to move forward in the will of the Lord. We cannot dwell in the history of yesterday. Our sins are forgiven through Christ Jesus! We must confess any shortcomings and get back on track in every area that God has assigned us to.

* Do **THAT** which the Lord revealed to you.
* Open **THAT** dance studio.
* Write **THAT** book.
* Host **THAT** conference.
* Establish **THAT** business.
* Choreograph **THAT** dance.
* Design **THAT** garment.
* Develop **THAT** website.
* Do **THAT** thing without further delay or fear!

If you have not yet taken the time to write the vision plainly, do it today! Stop promising tomorrow what should have been done yesterday. Run with joy the race that is set before you. Your blessing is in your obedience to the will of God concerning your life.

In obedience to God, lift up your hands, and the hands of someone else. Wait for the Lord's timing and follow His direction with purity. Working together as one Body, we all obtain the victory for Kingdom advancement. We were not connected with others to obtain the victory alone. Let us exalt His name together!

> *Strengthen the weak hands,*
> *And make firm*
> *the feeble knees.*
>
> *Say to those who are*
> *fearful-hearted,*
> *"Be strong, do not fear!*
> *Behold, your God will come with vengeance,*
> *With the recompense of God;*
> *He will come and save you."*

- Isaiah 35:3-4

CAUSE 9

What Every Kingdom Dancer Should Know

It is amazing to me how little so many in the church know of the Word of God for themselves. Even more astounding are the number of dancers in the Body who are unaware of the many instances of dance in the Bible, church protocol, garment basics, music selection, and so much more! Although there are no concrete "rules" that each and every dance ministry must abide by, the practical wisdom that has been gleaned over the years is something to be sought after and shared.

KNOWLEDGE

It is imperative that each movement ministry take time to examine the Scriptures concerning dance. I often teach at dance conferences and rarely get more than two answers when I ask the question, "Who danced in the Bible?" Most are familiar with David, and it often ends there. Other chapters of this book have helped us discover the names of these additional dancers, but reading alone will not suffice. There is a difference between reading about something and actually knowing it. Dedicating regular review time during rehearsal will help dancers to retain the knowledge of the Scriptures.

Each dancer should also have a thorough understanding of the leadership structure to which they report. For the solo dancer, this may be a much smaller accountability system in which he or she may report to a Pastor or other leader in the local church. For larger groups, there is usually a key leader who reports to the Pastor or other key ministry leader. As groups grow in number, it may be necessary to establish additional servant leaders to help bear the load. For example, in Reign Dance Company, we have an Artistic Director, Technical Trainer, Choreography Coach, Finance Administrator, Keeper of the Wardrobe, and Team Leaders arranged by age group. This allows us to operate more efficiently and reduces the potential for burnout for any one particular person on the ministry team. Clearly communicate whatever the structure is to the unit so that everyone understands who does what.

The Bible reminds us, *"...to know them which labour among you..."* (1 Thessalonians 5:12- KJV). We should make a sincere effort to know fellow dance ministries in our communities and in our nations. Not only does this give us an opportunity to come together as co-laborers, we may also glean some wisdom from key leaders who may be able to guide us in the right direction through experience and practical application of what has already been established concerning the ministry of movement.

With advances in technology, book publishing, abundant websites, and dance conferences, researching ministries and leaders of distinction should not be difficult. A standard search engine can yield results by plugging in the words praise dance, worship dance, liturgical dance, Christian dance, and so forth. Different word options will result in different listings, but the point is to have a good grasp on what is happening around us as well as throughout the world.

GETTING PERSONAL

There are some things that each dancer must take responsibility for on his or her own. If we proclaim to be ministers of the Gospel through dance, we must confess Jesus as Lord and Savior! How can we share a personal experience about someone we've never met? When we allow others to dance about Jesus without receiving Him, we encourage them to be hypocrites. I have learned not just to take someone's word for it. When dancers say that they are saved, I ask them what that means. If there is no clear understanding, it should be explained again and established, if necessary.

When a person expresses a desire to join a dance ministry, there should be an inherent

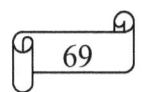

rhythm and an ability to move. The arts attract people for different reasons, and the dance ministry is no exception. Although there are times when an individual may be nervous or unsure of choreography, a chronic inability to capture movement or retain combinations may indicate an inability to continue serving as a dancer in this area.

Beyond the dance, there is a need for discipleship. Movement itself will not be enough to sustain us in absence of the continued study of the Word of God. The Lord has given me many visions of unique choreography and visions through the knowledge of His Word. There also must come a time when we are willing to put our gifts and talents to the side and make sure that serving the Lord with our whole hearts is our most important priority. The Lord tells us that if we love Him, we will keep His commandments (John 14:15). We cannot minister dances about loving God and break every ordinance in the Book.

In addition to what we do privately, what we exhibit publicly must also be governed with care. Many social networking websites allow us to post our thoughts, pictures, activities, and more for the world to see. When we claim to dance for the Lord and display vulgar images, foul language, and other behavior that does not give glory to God, we compromise the effectiveness and reputations of our ministries.

Even at home, we should have a good reputation with our friends and family, local churches, and our communities.

Neglecting our responsibilities in the name of ministry means that we need to revisit good stewardship and practice time management. If we create bills and neglect to pay them regularly but travel frequently to events and buy elaborate garments, we are not serving as good examples of Godly principles. What we do on a personal level definitely impacts our ministries. Let us be wiser in these areas and seek God's wisdom for improvement in the places we need to become better.

PRESENTATION

How we present ourselves both before the Lord and His people matters. "Come as you are" is not in the Bible, though when we first come to the Lord, He will receive us in whatever state we may be. After we receive Him into our lives, we are NEW creatures in Christ! There should be a transformation that starts in the mind and works its way through us and outward.

For dancers, physical appearance and personal hygiene serve as part of our ministry. Hair should be properly cared for and appropriate to the ministry presentation at all times. Hair that has not been washed and appears dirty or unkempt without a cause will adversely affect the message that we are trying to share with others. If the dance leader sets an order for all of the dancers to follow, then all of the dancers must submit and support the mandate given. Although we all have personal preferences about which hairstyles look best on us, we must be humble enough to place the message of the Gospel over our own vanity.

Dancers must have clean bodies! I cannot express this enough. Being that we often are in close proximity to others mandates that we not be offensive in their presence. When possible, we should aim to wash or shower as close to the time of ministry as we can. When we do not have that option, carrying small towels, wipes, and refreshers will also be a help. Additionally, deodorant, lotion, perfumes, colognes, mints or oils should be kept on hand when the occasion merits. We must also exercise wisdom in this area. Too much perfume or cologne could also be a distraction and deodorant may find its way onto our garments.

Jewelry can be a point of contention in dance ministry, but safety is of the utmost concern. If a dance leader requests that no jewelry be worn or that earrings and rings be kept to a minimum, unity must prevail. If the jewelry being worn serves as a distraction or safety hazard, we may compromise the message or be placing our own desires ahead of the needs of others.

Our hands and feet are also essential components of our ministry presentations. Many dance styles require shoes and some may call for the removal of them. Either way, we must keep our feet in good condition so that we can dance for His glory. Neglecting our toenails can result in difficulty dancing, damaged shoes, or foot infections. Keeping our hands and feet maintained will assist us with health and safety. Fingernail polish that is more expressive artwork than ministry motivated may act as a deterrent for the message being delivered.

One of the most important elements of our presentations includes the garments of ministry. While I will not expound on a teaching here, I will say that there are some basic things that we must consider when wearing them. Our undergarments should remain under our garments! This includes the ability to see any underwear through barely-there dresses, ill-fitting garments, or wearing bold patterns or brightly colored undergarments underneath light colors.

Each garment worn should be appropriate to the message being ministered through the dance piece. We must also consider the backgrounds of people to whom we are sent to minister and make needed adjustments in wisdom. Modesty is always in order. Caring for our garments properly will help us to avoid being embarrassed by holes, stains, snags, tears, or other items needing attention. We should make it a practice to examine our garments both before and after we dance to keep them in the best condition possible.

Music selection is a major part of what we do. Just because we are inspired by another ministry piece does not mean that we should obtain the same music and render our own versions of it. We must always allow the Lord to lead us to the message that He wants to give to His people. Inspiration does not merit imitation!

When presenting our music to sound engineers, we should always aim to present a clean format of our song on a CD or digital music device. If we present a CD, it should be clearly labeled and tested for accuracy. When using devices, we should always make sure that they are fully charged and that there is minimal potential for error. How embarrassing would it be if the movement minister handed over a device including songs that did not glorify God and one happened to be played by mistake? It is a good idea to obtain materials and devices that are exclusively set apart for the ministry.

CORPORATELY

If the ministry is dedicated to praise and worship, each dancer must be comfortable with these expressions. Without a teaching and understanding of praise and worship, most people will not automatically be radical for

Christ. We must reinforce our understanding of praise and worship with practical application. Waiting to practice this during church services is not enough! Ongoing praise and worship should also take place on a regular basis in our rehearsals as well as in our individual homes.

Prayer should take place at every gathering. Depending on one person to pray for everyone is not a good model for a team. Although there may be those assigned to intercede for the ministry on a regular basis, each team member, including children, can be taught to pray effectually and fervently. Also, devoting regular study time to the Word and other supplementary study books will help enhance the ministry and promote team unity.

Each ministry and team member should notify leadership when absent or discuss outside ministry invitations when appropriate. The absence of one person may impact the ministry, but should never hinder it. Each person in the unit must understand the importance of his or her position and be faithful to the assignment. If the season has changed and a dancer can no longer keep the commitment, there should be a peaceful conversation about the scheduled departure and it should be handled in love.

BASIC PROTOCOL

Your gift will make room for you, so there is no need to contact others to request to dance on

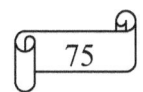

programs. Although many have adopted the practice of sending video "resumes" and requesting to dance or teach for a gathering, the doors that we open for ourselves will be the same ones we will have to work to keep open! Many conference and event hosts invite people to minister based on spiritual relationships and fruitfulness in a particular ministry. If we try to advance ourselves when it is not time for us to go forth, we can end up hindering our ministries and stunting our growth. Wait on the Lord!

How we conduct ourselves before ministry makes a difference. Not only must we be conscious of the surroundings that we create, we must also be careful of those created by others. If we are listening to music that does not glorify God in our cars on the way to ministry, we are sending mixed messages to our own spirits! As a great practice, we may want to avoid unrelated conversations, arguments, or other distractions before we prepare to dance before the Lord.

Arriving on time will be a great asset to our ministries. As a matter of fact, we should arrive early whenever possible. This allows us to discern the spiritual atmosphere of a place and respect it or have an opportunity to change it for the better. When we have a habit of running late, we not only place unneeded stress on ourselves, we also spread worry to the event host, other leaders, and related staff members.

Wherever we go to minister, we should understand how to conduct ourselves while we are there. In the interest of excellence, we should strategically plan our entrances and exits as well as observe pulpit or platform etiquette. Entering the area we are to dance in an orderly fashion will help minimize any confusion that may result when taking our places before the song begins. Depending on the church or venue, there may be areas that the dancers may not be allowed to dance. We should ask about this in advance. When exiting the platform after ministry, the dancers should know if they should return to their seats immediately or follow other instructions. Yes, little details matter. When we operate in excellence, promotion will follow.

Regarding respect for the ministry, we should not make a practice of dancing for a service and then immediately leaving afterward to go dance for another event or just because our portion of the service is complete. Even though there are instances where programs run beyond the expected timeframe, if we are always the ministry who dances and dashes, our reputations will suffer because of it.

While we are seated or experiencing the ministry of others we should adopt great standards of discipline. Excessive conversation or joking may be a distraction to our neighbors. Frequent trips to the restroom or other visible distractions can also be avoided by preparing for our needs ahead of time. Our disposition for the duration of a service or gathering is as much a part of our ministries as the piece itself. Let's not behave in any manner that would contradict the Gospel message delivered through us.

In addition to study, training, protocol and discipline, we must continue to stay aware of any new developments in our area of ministry. There are many dance ministry and worship books, websites, garment providers, worship tool makers, and other resources available to us. The best way to gather this information is by referral as well as research.

We can allow ourselves to be hindered by our own imaginations or lack thereof. Every Kingdom dancer must know that the dance itself is only one portion of our ministries. Dance may be the vehicle, but it is not the destination. We must strive to make our service to God and others a lifestyle and not just another activity.

CAUSE 10

The Spirit of Haman

"Now all these things happened to them as examples, and they were written for our admonition, upon whom the ends of the ages have come. Therefore let him who thinks he stands take heed lest he fall. No temptation has overtaken you except such as is common to man; but God is faithful, who will not allow you to be tempted beyond what you are able, but with the temptation will also make the way of escape, that you may be able to bear it."

-1 Corinthians 10:11-13

Sometimes the Lord will give me a message to deliver that is not easy. This is one of those times. The Lord revealed to me the practice of "planting flags" taking place with many ministries (See the Cause entitled **"X" Marks the Spot**). This practice includes those who invite themselves to minister in various places to extend their professional and ministry resumes. Books, conferences, websites, and flooded itineraries do not equal "Sent by God."

There is another alarm ringing in the atmosphere that I must sound. **ALERT! <u>God is Sovereign.</u>** Let us be careful not to harshly condemn fellow dancers and ministries we may disagree with. When we become judge, jury and executioner of those we may have "issues" with, we can begin to operate in what may be referred to as "The Spirit of Haman."

In the book of Esther, Haman's character is revealed and serves as an example to us of what NOT to do. We can all become "Haman" if we are not careful! If you are suddenly promoted, PRAY! If you believe that you are "THE" authority in a certain area or subject matter, HUMBLE YOURSELF! If you feel the urge to lay your stamp of approval or denial on the ministry or work of another, **STOP RIGHT THERE!**

> *"Lift not up your horn on high: speak not with a stiff neck. For promotion cometh neither from the east, nor from the west, nor from the south. But God is the judge: he putteth down one, and setteth up another. -Psalm 75:5-7 (KJV)*

Right after Haman was promoted by King Ahasuerus in Esther Chapter 3, he began to think that he was worthy to be praised. After all, the king himself gave him his blessing! How many of us have thought that we were important because of the "names" we were affiliated with? "Well, 'Such and Such' said that I was anointed... Prophetess 'So and So' laid her hands on me and said that I was called to the nations... Renowned Bishop 'Who's Who' personally ordained me..." The trap is now set. Indicators of the spirit of Haman:

Desire to be Recognized/Honored

"When Haman saw that Mordecai did not bow or pay him homage, Haman was filled with wrath."
                                              - Esther 3:5

Have you ever been on program after ministry and anticipated the moment your name was to be called? "How loud and how long will they clap for me? Will they shout out my name? Will they tell me how powerfully the Lord used me, His chosen vessel for such a time as this? Why did they not invite ME to speak at that conference? I am a child of the King!"

"Humble yourselves in the sight of the Lord, and He will lift you up."   - James 4:10

Elitist Mentality

"But he disdained to lay hands on Mordecai alone, for they had told him of the people of Mordecai. Instead, Haman sought to destroy all the Jews who were throughout the whole kingdom of Ahasuerus- the people of Mordecai."
                                              –Esther 3:6

Excuse me, but I am sick and tired of the "sorority mentality" that I see in some of our dance ministry circles! Because Mordecai did not bow down to Haman, Haman sought to banish all those who were affiliated with Mordecai! This takes me back to childhood scenarios: "I am not gonna be your friend if you

81

are her friend. I do not like her." Lord have mercy on us right now!

I speak this in love: Just because your relationship did not work out with someone else does not mean that the other person is evil or not a child of God. The Lord knows us better that we know ourselves. Honestly, I love so hard that if the Lord did not remove me from some of my past relationships, I would not be walking in my destiny right now! I would still be holding onto *that* relationship, *that* dance ministry, *that* Pastor, *that* church, and be walking completely outside of the will of God!

Remember the children of Israel? This Scripture always blesses me when I feel rejected: *"But the LORD hardened Pharaoh's heart, and he did not let the children of Israel go."* (Exodus 10:20) The Lord wants to demonstrate His power through you. Do not worry about those who seem to turn their backs on you. Do not take it personally or as a setback. Stay in the place of humility and do not allow your emotions to take over the workings of the Spirit. God is in complete control!

Elitists also think that you should do things EXACTLY the way that they would. Look at Haman's comment here: *Then Haman said to King Ahasuerus, "There is a certain people scattered and dispersed among the people in all the provinces of your kingdom; their laws are different from all other people's, and they do not keep the king's laws. Therefore it is not fitting for the king to let them remain."*

- Esther 3:8

I thank the Lord that I am fearfully and wonderfully made! This does not mean that we are not to follow Divine order. This does mean that God has the option to do as He sees fit. Our merciful God can use anything and anybody. Consider the donkey in 2 Peter 2:16, *"...but he was rebuked for his iniquity: a dumb donkey speaking with a man's voice restrained the madness of the prophet."* If You can use anything Lord, You can use (even) me!

Pride

"Then Haman told them of his great riches, the multitude of his children, everything in which the king had promoted him, and how he had advanced him above the officials and servants of the king. Moreover Haman said, "Besides, Queen Esther invited no one but me to come in with the king to the banquet that she prepared; and tomorrow I am again invited by her, along with the king. Yet all this avails me nothing, so long as I see Mordecai the Jew sitting at the king's gate."

- Esther 5:11-13

It is not ironic that Haman's name means "magnificent." (Strong's #2001) If we are not watchful, we can begin to believe the hype concerning our own ministries. When we begin to "read our own press" we can easily envision the glorious heights to which we can rise... dancing far above the clouds... and everyone else! Lord, help us not to be consumed with our own progress and forget that others are called just as we are. We are many members...

Are you wasting your time right now consumed with people? Time is precious! Invest that energy into doing the work that the Lord has called **you** to do. Too often we may be tempted to impress people when telling them of all of the conferences to which we are traveling, the miracles that God worked through us, or our years of training and biblical studies. Guess what? God does not care about that! Are you doing His will and obeying Him? Ask for a Holy Ghost check up right now!

Murderous/Vengeful

"So the king said, "Who is in the court?" Now Haman had just entered the outer court of the king's palace to suggest that the king hang Mordecai on the gallows that he had prepared for him." –Esther 6:4

Who are you murdering with your mouth today? I pray right now for clean hands and a pure heart in your life at this very moment. Even if you strongly believe that someone has sinned against you, is operating outside of the will of God, or any other issue, it is not your job to police them. Do not feed into this temptation. Vengeance is the Lord's. Jesus serves as our chief example in John 4:34: *"Jesus said to them, "My food is to do the will of Him who sent Me, and to finish His work."* We must place the Lord's will for our lives as our chief priority.

If you are involved in the planning of the demise of another, whether directly or indirectly, you are planning the downfall of yourself! Leave that ministry and that dancer in the Lord's hands. What is the more powerful testimony- that a ministry you have a problem with is destroyed, or that the Lord restores the ministry just as we are shown in the example of the prodigal son in Luke 15:11-32? Let the redemptive work of the Lord take place in the name of Jesus!

Self-Destructive

"When Haman told his wife Zeresh and all his friends everything that had happened to him, his wise men and his wife Zeresh said to him, 'If Mordecai, before whom you have begun to fall, is of Jewish descent, you will not prevail against him but will surely fall before him.'"

–Esther 6:12

85

Take heed unless you fall! Refuse to let the enemy gain a foothold in your ministry. Focus on the Lord and pleasing your Father in heaven. If the Lord has appointed you to be a watchman, WATCH! He did not call you to be a "hangman." Let us continue to take inventory regarding our motives in ministry. Are you sharing a testimony that is really a veiled noose to condemn another who may have hurt you in ministry? Are you reacting to past hurt by rejecting anything and everyone who may be associated with the one who hurt you? Have we gotten to the point in ministry where we cannot move beyond the hurt and embrace true healing?

I pray that we kill all of the traits of Haman in our lives this instant. I pray the Lord's forgiveness for every gallows that we may have erected against one another...

"Heavenly Father, bring the high places in our lives low. Re-turn us Lord in every pirouette and piqué turn. Reveal to us in movement the turning away from sin and the re-turn to righteousness. I pray that the Lord fill every void, heal every hurt, and restore every prodigal ministry back to the fold. I pray right now that the Lord has washed our hands and healed our hearts so that the spirit of Haman is laid to rest in our lives and ministries... in Jesus' name I pray. Amen."

CAUSE 11

"X" MARKS THE SPOT

"Let nothing be done through selfish ambition or conceit, but in lowliness of mind let each esteem others better than himself."

- Phillippians 2:3

As I take note of what is happening in many ministries, I am reminded of the TV show "The Amazing Race." It seems as though many ministries are racing to be the first to "arrive," mark a territory, claim a region, stake a claim, etc. The problem is something I refer to as "Planting a Flag." Historically, raising or planting a flag in a region signifies a territorial claim to victory. The issue is that the flag being raised is not that of Christ or the Kingdom, but the name of the individual or ministry itself.

As many have taken "Christ" out of Christmas and replaced it with "X-mas," I fear that this is not only happening during the holiday season. Many ministries have followed the popular trend of taking CHRIST out, and making the ministry name BIGGER than the name of Jesus. These **"INSERT YOUR NAME HERE"** Ministries may not even realize what is happening. When the namesake goes, so does the ministry! Often, I have ministered in dance and the emcee could not recall my name, but remarked on the message and ministry that went forth through the dance. Each time that this happens, I praise the Lord even more: *"He must increase, but I must decrease."* -John 3:30

<u>I must confess</u>: When I began in dance ministry, I wanted everyone to hear my opinion and experiences concerning "praise dance." I was overjoyed when we were booked each weekend of each month- a calendar full of "engagements!" We felt so ***anointed*** and became confident that our ministry was the benchmark of what God was doing in the movement ministries. As He lovingly does, God stepped right in and revealed to me the ugliness and truth of what was really happening: the ministry became my god, I placed my friendship and relationship with my dance partner above my relationship with my spouse, and everything that I *thought* was "order" was not God's order in my ambition to be "in ministry." I had to put the dance ministry on the altar of sacrifice, ask

my husband for forgiveness, and let the Lord teach me **His** ways anew. I thank Him for His correction and grace.

As the trend dictates, it seems as though every ministry wants to be on television, host radio broadcasts, win competitions and become famous. If the Lord has blessed you to have a great name and exposure, this is wonderful! If you are convinced that it is YOUR time to shine because you have served in dance ministry for several years, have a special revelation from the Lord that the WHOLE WORLD needs to hear, and YOU are going to be "the one" to minister uniquely throughout the nations, BEWARE! Do not be one of many who "went... but were not sent." Please, do not invite yourself to go out to minister because you think that you have something to impart. It is better to be invited. Doesn't the Word say that "Your gift will make room for you?" Unfortunately, too many of us are trying to make "room for our gifts."

Luke 14:8-11 warns us:

"When you are invited by anyone to a wedding feast, do not sit down in the best place, lest one more honorable than you be invited by him; and he who invited you and him come and say to you, 'Give place to this man,' and then you begin with shame to take the lowest place. But when you are invited, go and sit down in the lowest place, so that when he who invited you

comes he may say to you, 'Friend, go up higher.' Then you will have glory in the presence of those who sit at the table with you. For whoever exalts himself will be humbled, and he who humbles himself will be exalted."

Promotion comes from the Lord. If you have invited yourself to teach and are anxious to get on program to dance or minister, please return to the position of humility immediately. Ask the Lord to reveal to you if you have tried to "Plant Your Flag" in a territory that He did not assign to you. There are many members of the Body, and we must not desire to operate in a way or place that we are not specifically appointed or ready to handle.

When was the last time that you supported a dance conference or event in which you were not named as a speaker or dancer? When did you last volunteer to serve or be a resource to a ministry that you were not personally vested in? Have you written or called a ministry lately just to let them know that they have been a blessing or inspiration during your ministry journey? If you have planted a flag in a territory that says "I Ministered Here," I encourage you to dispose of your own logo-emblazoned standard, and replace it with the banner that reads: **Jehovah Nissi** *"The-Lord-My-Banner."* -Exodus 17:15

CAUSE 12

MMMM!

Mission-Ministry-Music-Movement

*"The fruit of the righteous is a tree of life,
and he who wins souls is wise."*
— Proverbs 11:30

We must understand that there is a strategy to soul-winning and ministry. When we are trained, informed, and equipped, we can make a greater impact as ministers of movement. Being ignorant of the needs of people as we stand before them will prove to be a fruitless experience. Ministry is service. The strategies contained here only serve as thinking points for you and your ministry. Following the Lord's leading will always result in an effective impact in the lives of His people.

As we prepare our pieces, we can consider the MMMM strategy when selecting songs and movements that will convey the appropriate message for the group we are assigned to. The Mission-Ministry-Music-Movement strategy will give us a big picture approach to ministry. This formula will also help us to ensure that we are not dancing from a self-centered standpoint, but that we always consider the impact that our ministries will have on others in the process.

MMMM!

MISSION
(Source: Merrian-Webster.com)

A ministry commissioned by a religious organization to propagate its faith or carry on humanitarian work

Those in the ministry of movement must be accountable. Accountability will protect us from operating as "lone rangers" and provide balance in our ministries. Obedience to God includes submitting to wise counsel.

For dance ministries that exist inside of a local church, this accountability system may include a Pastor, ministry leader, or advisor. The dancer usually reports any ministry-related activities and challenges to this counselor and is open to receiving feedback, direction, correction, and encouragement.

A course of sermons and services given to convert the un-churched or quicken Christian faith

True movement ministers dance with a specific assignment to complete. This includes reaching people who are professed believers as well as those yet to accept Jesus Christ as Lord and Savior. Each dancer must have an accurate understanding of the Gospel message and have the heart of a servant. Merely having a desire to dance will not impact lives eternally without the Word of God in motion.

A body of persons sent to perform a service or carry on an activity

This body of persons includes dancers, supporters, assistants, and anyone else that assists the solo dancer or team in spreading the Word through movement. We must be selected by God to perform this activity as a ministry. There are many in the Body today who desire to launch themselves for the purpose of personal profit and monetary gain. Those commissioned for this mission receive an assignment to do so.

A specific task with which a person or a group is charged

Each ministry must have a specific objective to accomplish. This mission must be understood in advance, and may occasionally be altered as circumstances change. Thorough training will allow each dancer to be able to adjust the mission as the needs of the people change or a shift in events prevents ministering the original song selected. At times, the Spirit may totally change the direction of a service.

There must be a clear mission each time the ministry of movement takes place. Dancers are sent on assignment, are accountable to the established leadership, and must choose to remain teachable. A clear understanding of this mission will result in a more effective unit of service.

MINISTRY

The act or process of ministering

Many dancers mistakenly think that ministry begins and ends with the song being presented. The truth is that service is a lifestyle and includes how we treat observers, families, and fellow ministry members. Movement is only one way that we minister to others. We can negate the positive effects of ministry if we compromise the ministry in any way.

A person or thing through which something is accomplished

The Lord uses individuals and groups of people for ministry. For dancers, our ministry must accomplish the work for which we were created. If the dance ministry is not formed to meet a specific need in the congregation, neighborhood, larger community, or the world, then we are merely another group gathering with a common interest, but without a need to exist.

MUSIC

A musical accompaniment

For many dancers, this is the piece of music to which we minister. This is often in the form of pre-recorded music (compact discs and digital storage devices), live instrumentation, or live vocal accompaniment. This may require amplified sound, musicians, or microphones for

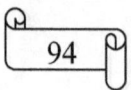

the intended message to be clearly heard and understood.

A distinctive type or category of music

For ministry, our songs are typically categorized as Gospel or Christian music. These include songs of praise, worship, testimony, prayer, and biblically-based lyrics. Inspirational music is not the same as Gospel or Christian music! Though there are songs that can be encouraging or uplifting that may inspire us, the "good news" without Jesus or praises that are not rendered to God are simply songs.

Those who desire to become true ministers through dance must make sure that the songs selected are able to be cross-referenced in the Word of God. Just because someone else has labeled a song in the Gospel or Christian categories does not mean that it must not pass the litmus test. We must study to make sure that our music is theologically sound and can be supported by the Scriptures.

MOVEMENT

A particular instance or manner of moving

Movement can include the style of dance through which we convey the message, a combination of styles, the dance piece itself, or the allotted time that we are to minister through movement. Often, Christian dance is set apart from other dance styles not only by the type of music selected, but by the movements used. Often, movements that are considered seductive or expose the body as a focal point are avoided.

A series of organized activities working toward an objective

Hear this: Our dances must be organized for a purpose! This work does not begin when we take a platform, but in the training and rehearsal times for our ministries. Disorganized, chaotic groupings and movements send a message of confusion more than they promote the Gospel. We must be clear while we are engaging in dances so that the message is not hindered.

An organized effort to promote or attain an end

The after effects of our ministries must also be considered as we move the Gospel forward. We must always check to make sure that we are not promoting ourselves or our ministries more than the goodness of God. What happens when the movement ceases? Are others compelled to praise or worship? Is the invitation to give one's life to Christ an option? Can believers and new converts be referred to a church or support system that will help them with their needs? Dance ministers cannot be uninformed in these areas. Even if a select group of people or ministry leaders are appointed to this task, care should be taken to make sure that all of the elements of ministry are in place and complete.

Now that we have discovered the formula for MISSION-MINISTRY-MUSIC-MOVEMENT, we will now review several scenarios common to dance ministry to test out this formula for victory each and every time. Wisdom must be exercised, but conventional human methodology cannot replace the direction of the Holy Spirit. The more that guesswork can be removed from ministry, the greater our capacity to obey God at every turn.

Survey the Land!

Before we accept invitations to dance, it would be wise to ask some standard questions about the event to include available space, sound system capabilities, time restrictions, garment expectations, the type of audience expected (age, beliefs, etc.), and any other details that may be needed to render a safe and effective movement piece (number of aisles, ceiling height, type of flooring, etc.).

WORSHIP SERVICES
Sunday Services, Bible Studies

Land Survey: Generally takes place in an enclosed building or designated space. For church-based dance ministries, this space is generally familiar and is used most often. When visiting churches, the configurations may be much different than what is customary. Dancers should be trained to be flexible when moving in an unfamiliar setting. Early arrival will assist with any adjustments that may need to be made after arriving at the location.

Mission: Demonstrate the Word of God in motion. Support the pulpit with dances that highlight pastoral teachings. Welcome the presence of the Lord. Cause others to be "moved."

Ministry: Directed to the general church congregation. This may include both saved and unsaved persons of different ages and backgrounds in the same location at the same time.

Music: Should flow with the service and represent the "personality" of the host. The message of the dance ministry should not openly conflict with the teachings of the leadership. Generally includes songs of worship, praise, celebration, battle, and testimony.

Movement: Open to interpretation. The dance should "depict a memorable story" while being able to be clearly understood by the congregation in attendance.

THEMATIC SERVICES
Concerts, Anniversary Services, Ministry Special Services, Etc.

Land Survey: Thematic services usually take place in churches, hotels, corporate meeting facilities, banquet halls, community centers, etc.

>*Mission:* Provide a visual demonstration of the Word. Encourage, edify, and uplift. Demonstrate the theme in action, if possible, or capture the spirit of the intended message of the event for agreement with the theme.

>*Ministry:* May include the guest(s) of honor as well as the general congregation. Ministry may be directed towards both saved and unsaved persons of different ages and cultures in attendance.

>*Music:* A specific theme may be chosen but it is not always possible to match the theme without compromising the sincerity of the ministry. As much as is possible, songs selected should include words that agree with the general intention of the theme or be related to the occasion. If the event is a celebration, then celebratory songs should be considered.

>*Movement:* Should match the message of the music, but is not limited to one distinct style. In some congregations, a

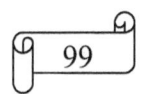

more traditional style may be preferred over contemporary movement depending on the denomination or traditions. Know before you go!

BIRTHDAY CELEBRATIONS

Then an opportune day came when Herod on his birthday gave a feast for his nobles, the high officers, and the chief men of Galilee.

And when Herodias' daughter herself came in and danced, and pleased Herod and those who sat with him, the king said to the girl, "Ask me whatever you want, and I will give it to you."
                                    -Mark 6:21-22

There are some who use this biblical instance as a reason to ban dance from the church. Throughout the Scriptures, we can read about instances of dance being used to glorify God, as celebration, and also for idol worship. This does not mean that we are not to use dance as a way to minister to others. We can learn from these examples that we must distinguish between different types of dances so that we do not fall into disobedience.

King Herod allowed Herodias' daughter to dance before him and an audience of his friends at his birthday celebration. Enamored, he extended her favor in granting whatever request she desired to be fulfilled. As we dance in the presence of our King, His favor is extended to us as we make our petitions known to Him. In the case of Herodias' daughter, her mother instructed her to request the execution of John the Baptist. Herodias' daughter danced the dance of death. We must seek to move in such a way that gives life to those who witness us!

Land Survey: Common locations for birthday celebrations include hotel ballrooms, banquet halls, community centers, private residences, parks, and other open spaces.

> *Mission:* Encourage celebrant. Celebrate the purpose of life in Christ.

> *Ministry:* Is often focused on the honoree. The impact often extends to party guests, food servers, caterers, parking lot attendants, DJs, etc. Ask the anticipated age range and background of the majority of the invited attendees to be better prepared for ministry.

> *Music:* Selections often include songs of thanksgiving, testimony, and celebration of life. Depending on the person, a specific type of music may be requested. Make sure to resist the temptation to compromise. If the Lord has not designed you or your group to dance to secular pieces or selections that do not fit the personality of your ministry, obey Him!

MMMM!

> **Movement:** Various dance techniques may be employed. Depending on the location, make sure that your footwear is able to be worn safely and your movements can be done with minimal potential for injury (i.e. dancing on concrete or rocky surfaces). Be sure to test the platform or flooring before dancing to make any adjustments.

WEDDINGS & ANNIVERSARIES

Husbands, love your wives, just as Christ also loved the church and gave Himself for her.
-Ephesians 5:25

Beloved, let us love one another,
for love is of God; and everyone who loves is born of God and knows God.

He who does not love does not know God, for God is love.

-I John 4:7-8

Movement ministry at weddings is becoming very common. Navigating nuptials should not be taken lightly! There are many in attendance at weddings that may not come to church or have never witnessed ministry in motion. Prayer and wisdom must be in operation for effective ministry at weddings.

Land Survey: It is a good idea to view the location in advance. If there is a rehearsal, this is a great occasion to work out any challenges that can be foreseen. When initially invited, find out if the dance will take place during the ceremony or reception. If dancing is taking place during the vows, knowing what comes before and after the dance may help with entrances and exits. Weddings often occur in church sanctuaries, hotel Ballrooms, private yachts, community centers, private residences, beaches, and other open spaces. Some of these spaces can be very confined. Dancing for the reception during a meal can be very distracting to a seasoned dance minister. Ask questions ahead of time to be properly prepared.

Mission: Demonstrate the love of God. Encourage right relationships. Proclaim blessings over the couple.

Ministry: Primarily to the bride and groom or married couple for wedding anniversaries. Also includes the wedding party, invited guests, DJ, wedding coordinator, hired staff, valets, etc. Many may come to a wedding that do not attend a local church on a regular basis. This is a great opportunity for restoration!

Music: Should highlight the love of God as the center of true love. If you have committed to serving in ministry, using secular music may be a compromise. Be careful of accepting weddings because of monetary offerings. It may not be wise for the dance minister to get out on the floor after ministry to continue the festivities by demonstrating the latest dance craze or indulging in alcohol. Often, a bride or groom may request a specific song. Whatever the case, be in line with God's design for your ministry at all times. If you cannot, do not!

Movement: We may want to limit overly complicated movement during sacred ceremonies. We may be surrounded by elaborate floral arrangements and décor, and must take safety into consideration. Dancing too close to the bride or groom may also be awkward if not handled with care. Always seek God for each ceremony concerning the appropriate way to minister for these occasions.

COMMUNITY OUTREACH & EVANGELISM

And He said to them, "Go into all the world and preach the gospel to every creature.
-Mark 16:15

Service to the community can be done through evangelistic outreach efforts. There is no limit to "dancing in the expanse" except those that are unlawful or need permits. The key to organizing successful outreach efforts is to plan far in advance and to fully research the opportunities and the challenges of participating in them.

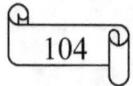

Land Survey: Outreach can happen in parking lots, open fields, public parks, shopping malls, community events, amateur and professional sporting events, fashion shows, and more! With permission, there are pretty much no limits to outreach. Of course, we must observe local ordinances regarding sound, event permits, and businesses that may be impacted by our efforts. Make every effort to forecast all logistics when organizing an outreach event.

Mission: We must always demonstrate the Word of God! Our goal is to reach the lost and to encourage the believer.

Ministry: Includes people from all walks of life and beliefs. Outreach is often cross-cultural and multi-generational. Some public locations may impose restrictions (i.e. no preaching or proselytizing on the premises) while permitting the name of Jesus to be used openly in the songs.

Music: Often includes a variety of styles and may speak of salvation, hope, love, and restoration. Songs should be prayed over and selected with context in mind. Songs that sound very similar to popular music may draw a crowd, but the message may be missed if the beat has been borrowed from the latest popular music charts. This may incite the crowd to dance more than listen to the message being shared.

Movement: Is often varied and can include many other participating groups. This is a great occasion to incorporate flags, banners, and streamers as visuals to attract others to the center of activity. Take care using these on a windy day and make sure to review safety with those who will be using these tools during ministry.

HOSPITALS & NURSING HOMES

*So they went out and preached
that people should repent.*

And they cast out many demons, and anointed with oil many who were sick, and healed them.
-Mark 6:12-13

Ministry in hospitals and nursing homes is becoming familiar territory to many movement ministries. At the time of sickness, many people are more open to faith and desire to be healed. Although some may never recover from their sickness, it is important to provide hope to those who are present.

Land Survey: Is often a designated space in a care facility. The dance space provided may be in a community room or common gathering area. Depending on the facility, there may be space restrictions or sound limitations. Use wisdom in the garments selected for ministry. The environment may be very cold and provide physical challenges for the dancer's limbs.

Mission: To minister healing, health, hope, recovery, and faith in God.

Ministry: Primarily to patients, but includes visitors, facility vendors, family members and hospital staff.

Music: Songs of healing, testimony, endurance, and encouragement. Follow the leading of the Holy Spirit.

Movement: May need to be adjusted due to space limitations or configuration. Pray, and ask the staff, about choreography that involves touching the sick or includes physical contact. Movement should be led by the Holy Spirit and match the spiritual gifting of the person dancing.

CORRECTIONAL FACILITIES

I, Paul, write this greeting in my own hand. Remember my chains. Grace be with you.
                                    -Colossians 4:18 (NIV)

We must not approach ministry with haughty spirits or pre-determined prejudices. Although many have ended up incarcerated for past mistakes, there are several inmates who sincerely love God and also minister to other

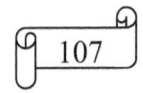

prisoners among them. In order to minister in prisons, you may need to undergo a background check. This may or may not be stringent based on the security level of the prison and the warden in charge. Be sure to clear any outstanding items on record, not only to avoid becoming an inmate, but to represent in a way that does not compromise your assignment.

Land Survey: Prison Facility Designated Space. The space may be expansive or confined. Try to gather as many details in advance as possible, but be prepared for a variety of options. Some prisons place restrictions on what can be worn (colors and styles must not be similar to inmate attire) and garments or props may need to be approved in advance.

> *Mission:* Deliver the Word of God. Encourage and comfort. Target the lost and encourage the believer.

> *Ministry:* Inmates, prison staff, visitors in passing, and fellow dance ministry members! Ministry in prison can be a life-changing and emotional experience. Even those designated to minister should remain open to receiving ministry as well.

> *Music:* Songs that highlight the Gospel, songs of hope, songs of restoration, praise and worship songs.

Movement: Many dance disciplines may be welcomed in a cross-cultural setting. Move with liberty in spite of bondage!

CELEBRATIONS OF LIFE

Also known as funerals, homegoing services, life celebrations, burial services, and wakes, many dancers are being requested to minister hope and encouragement to families and friends. We must be sensitive in these environments as emotions run high and hearts are open. This may be one of the most delicate occasions in which a dance minister may participate.

"For we know that if our earthly house, this tent, is destroyed, we have a building from God, a house not made with hands, eternal in the heavens."
-2 Corinthians 5:1

Land Survey: Primarily conducted at churches, funeral homes, and gravesites.

Mission: To comfort the mourning and encourage right relationships.

Ministry: Towards loved ones that include relatives, friends, co-workers, associates, and more. Also includes staff on location. These services may attract people that NEVER come to church or do not believe in Jesus as Lord. What an opportunity to remind them of God's love and care. We want them to "Come Home" too!

Music: Should encourage, but not overwhelm the people with emotion. We must be sensitive to the atmosphere. Always seek God about what He needs for specific families and causes of death.

Movement: There may be many challenges due to floral arrangements, casket placement, and proximity of seating. Movement in these instances is usually graceful, but can be open depending on the personality of the individual and the family. Adhere to the requests of the family as much as possible and be attentive to their needs.

EQUIPPED FOR MINISTRY

All members of the movement ministry should be trained to lead others to Christ. For safety and accountability, train them to minister two at a time to one person. You may desire to designate an evangelism team or leader to handle extra special circumstances.

We do not want to lose even one person! If we are strategic and proceed with wisdom, we will win souls, touch lives, and impact this world.

But what does it say? "The word is near you, in your mouth and in your heart" (that is, the word of faith which we preach):

That if you confess with your mouth the Lord Jesus and believe in your heart that God has raised Him from the dead, you will be saved.

For with the heart one believes unto righteousness, and with the mouth confession is made unto salvation.

For the Scripture says, "Whoever believes on Him will not be put to shame."

For there is no distinction between Jew and Greek, for the same Lord over all is rich to all who call upon Him.

For "whoever calls on the name of the LORD shall be saved."

-Romans 10:8-13

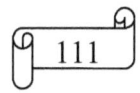

111

THE EFFECT...

For some, taking a stand may be easier than learning how to bow in His presence. I am completely humbled and amazed by the great things that He has done. To say that my life is anything short of miraculous would be to give God too little credit.

It would have been easier to be a statistic, following a pre-determined path based on my history, demographics, and social status... but GOD! He has exceeded my every expectation, transformed my thoughts completely, pulled me out of the pit, and given me refuge under His wings.

For this cause I bow my knees... not because of His manifold blessings, but because of His goodness, grace, and mercy. I kneel in His presence to honor Him as LORD and Redeemer of my life. In humble adoration I submit, because He is worthy to receive my most sincere praise and my purest worship.

The ministry of movement has benefitted my life and that of so many others. Through dance, God has opened doors that I could have never walked through without His provision. I am eternally thankful for the vehicle He has chosen to get me to my destination by His will. For this cause I bow my knees... time and time again.

REKESHA PITTMAN

Rekesha has been in training for ministry from her youth. Whether singing, dancing, acting, or speaking publicly, the Lord has graced her to be able to stand before His congregation with boldness. Her intense desire for ministerial excellence has opened the doors for her to minister in both dance and teaching of the Word on a National and International level.

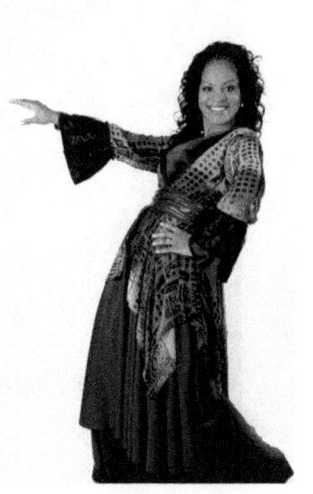

Rekesha is a teacher of the Word and serves as workshop facilitator, mentor, consultant, and intercessor for various dance ministries, churches, worship arts departments, and music ministries. She is married to Matthew Pittman, a dynamic musician and ministry supporter. Her innermost desire is that pleasing the Lord be the focus of service in ministry, and that worship is an essential component in the daily life of every believer in the Body of Christ.

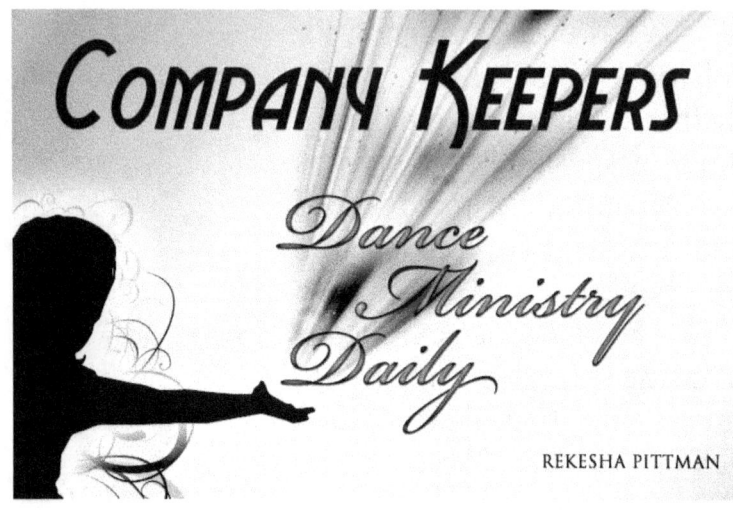
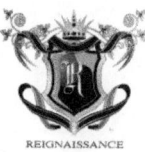

www.ingramcontent.com/pod-product-compliance
Lightning Source LLC
Chambersburg PA
CBHW072211170526
45158CB00002BA/546